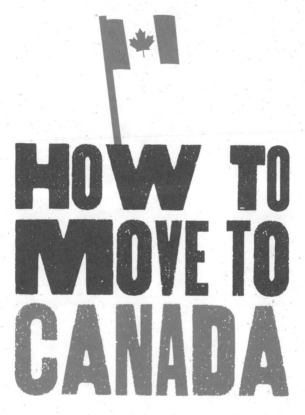

# HOW TO MOVE TO CANADA

## A Discontented American's
## Guide to Canadian Relocation

# ANDRÉ DU BROC

sourcebooks

Photo Credits for *How To Move to Canada*
USED THROUGHOUT: arm, urfinguss/Thinkstock; eagle, Tom Brakefield/Thinkstock; solid flag, RamCreativ/Thinkstock; grunge Canadian flag, korinoxe/Thinkstock; maple leaf, nubumbim/Thinkstock; CHAPTER 4: 1¢, 5¢, 10¢, and 25¢ coins, Zoonar RF/Thinkstock; 50¢ coin, Zedcor Wholly Owned/Thinkstock; $1 coin, Vitalily73/Thinkstock; $2 coin, michaklootwijk/Thinkstock; $5 and $50 bills, ppart/Thinkstock; $10 and $20 bills, John Hockin/Thinstock; $100 bill, RusFaz/Thinkstock; hands, Wavebreakmedia Ltd/Thinkstock; crown, leonello/Thinkstock; flag, Alexyndr/Thinkstock; podium, razihusin/Think stock; moose, Anagramm/Thinkstock; CHAPTER 5: flags, zak00/Thinkstock; maps, notviper/Thinkstock; CHAPTER 6: basket, miflippo/Thinkstock; bear, Azure-Dragon/Thinkstock; beer, MileA/Thinkstock; binoculars, Vitalii Hulai/Thinkstock; bird feeder, Ryan McVay/Thinkstock; boots, marekuliasz/Thinkstock; bowties, UroshPetrovic/Thinkstock; cans, Hemera Technologies/Thinkstock; clover, LiuSol/Thinkstock; cookie cutter, akiyoko/Thinkstock; donut, AlexRaths/Thinkstock; firewood, Givaga/Thinkstock; globe moodboard/Thinkstock; gloves, NAKphotos/Thinkstock; ketchup, scanrail/Thinkstock; pogo stick, Grzegorz Petrykowski/Thinkstock; rope, yanikap/Thinkstock; ski mask, joaninha777/Thinkstock; snorkel, abadonian/Thinkstock; snowshoes, Lilkin/Thinkstock; swiss knife, gemenacom/Thinkstock

This book is a work of humor and intended for entertainment purposes only.
All brand names and product names used in this book are trademarks, registered trademarks, or trade names of their respective holders. Sourcebooks, Inc., is not associated with any product or vendor in this book.

Published by Sourcebooks, Inc.
P.O. Box 4410, Naperville, Illinois 60567–4410
(630) 961-3900
Fax: (630) 961-2168
www.sourcebooks.com

Printed and bound in the United States of America.
VP 10 9 8 7 6 5 4 3 2 1

# CONTENTS

**V** INTRODUCTION

**1** CHAPTER 1:
Determining Your Best Entry Route

**21** CHAPTER 2:
Paperwork Is Not Terminal, but It Can
Feel That Way

**39** CHAPTER 3:
Learning How to Speak like a Canuk
(Which Means Canadian)

**55** CHAPTER 4:
Creating Canadian Pride

**77** CHAPTER 5:
But What Is Habitable in Canada?

**105** CHAPTER 6:
Packing Essentials and Syrup

**119** CHAPTER 7:
Making the Leap

**131** ABOUT THE AUTHOR

**132** ACTIVITIES ANSWER KEY

# INTRODUCTION

**W**ithout a doubt, as an ironclad patriot, you hold tightly to the ever-gleaming promise of the American dream. You know that with resilience, know-how, and a little old-fashioned elbow grease, you can accomplish just about anything your little flag-waving, red-white-and-blue heart desires.

Want to be an astronaut?—*That'll take some work, but don't see why not.*

Want to discover a cure for cancer?—*Good for you, you little do-gooder! Go for it!*

Want to write a book?—*I did it! You can too!*

No dream is too big, and in case you didn't know,

as a credit-card-carrying U.S. citizen, you are entitled to every one of those dreams coming true. That's what it means to be a proud American. Of course, when things don't go as planned—when NASA finds out you only joined so you could wear a space suit and post pics to Facebook, when the cancer research team dismisses you after finding out you have a two-pack-a-day habit, when your book is never picked up and you have to settle for writing a topical how-to manual instead— there's another American dream to be had. A dream that all good U.S. citizens keep in their subconscious. A dream that corporate types officiously refer to as "an exit plan." A dream that dare not speak its name, unless, of course, you're a media celebrity sharing your ever-so-relevant political views. That other American dream is, you guessed it, moving to Canada.

### HOW DID CANADA GET ITS NAME?

Originating from the St. Lawrence Iroquoian word *kanata* for "village," it was adopted by the first French settlers in the sixteenth century and just stuck. Leave it to the French to start a trend.

You're fed up with American politics and have threatened time and time again to pack up and go.

By purchasing this book, you have taken the first step toward realizing this dream. If you were gifted this book, then your relocation to Canada is part of someone else's dream. Either way, dreams are magical and a wish that your heart makes—at least according to Disney.

Before heading north, or to the right if you live in Alaska, carefully read through the advice offered in this user-friendly and completely analog guide to Canadian resettlement. In it you will find the answers to such questions as:

*What's a tuque, and what part of my body is it supposed to protect?*

*What's a Terry Fox, and is it on the endangered list? If not, when's open season?*

*What's a pogey, and can I be one when I grow up?*

You'll also learn all the ins and outs of becoming a Canadian citizen. So, to get you started down the right path in your great Canadian dream quest, here's an activity to whet your appetite for warm maple syrup and oozy poutine.

# COLOR THE FLAG OF YOUR NEW HOMELAND

## THE CANADIAN FLAG (A.K.A. THE MAPLE LEAF OR *L'UNIFOLIÉ* IF YOU WANT TO PASS AS A QUEBECER OR QUÉBÉCOIS)

Hint—you'll need a red crayon. That's all. Just a red one. Oh, and if you do a good job, don't brag. It's just not something a good Canadian would do.

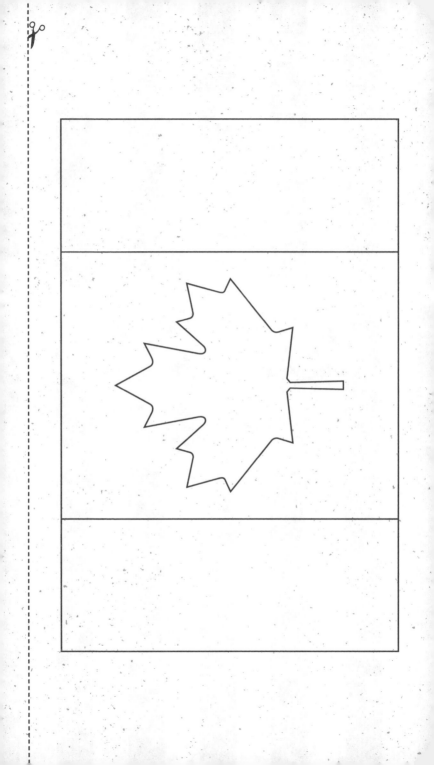

# 1

---

# DETERMINING YOUR BEST ENTRY ROUTE

I n your decision to move to Canada, you may consider yourself a promising pioneer of sorts, a naive newcomer, a self-confident settler, or even an enthusiastic ex-patriot; however, in legal terms, you are an alien going through the delightful and fun-filled process of immigration. That's right. Like it or not, you are now an immigrant. And being an alien immigrant seeking entry to a foreign country, you're required to jump through more hoops than a Chihuahua traveling in a Shriner's circus.

Lucky for you, this book explains some of the available options for establishing Canadian residency and a lot of what you'll need to know in order to complete the process without completely losing your will to live.

The first bit of maple-leaf-red tape you'll need

to untangle is obtaining a visa. A visa allows you to legally exist on Canadian soil and may even allow you to obtain employment while anxiously awaiting your permanent resident (PR) card, which grants you all the freedom and benefits enjoyed by your fellow Canadians with the exception of voting or holding a high-security job. Consider this a reality show of sorts: *So You Think You Can Be a Canadian?* Love your hair. Hope you win.

## GETTING YOUR PAPERS IN ORDER

Here's a handy-dandy list of some of the many documents you'll need before applying for your Canadian visa. Have fun gathering these. Make it a game. Kind of like a scavenger hunt devised by Ivan the Terrible and Courtney Love. Enjoy!

* **Your birth certificate.** Proof you exist and of where you were born. If you popped out of a birth canal on American soil, chances are you have one of these.

* **Your criminal record (a.k.a. police certificate).** Remember when your friends dared you to shoplift that bottle of Mad Dog 20/20 from the

Circle K when you were sixteen years old? Life is filled with such regrets, and there's a paper trail to remind you of them.

★ **Your medical records.** In a land of socialized health care, they really don't want to accept expensive sick people. Seriously, don't even cough during your entrance interview.

★ **Your passport.** You're a foreign national. This is a no-brainer. Don't have one? Get one! Don't know how? Go to USPS's website under international passports.

★ **Your tax records.** Thought you'd skip out of the States without paying your bill? Don't be a Sneaky Pete.

★ **Your marriage certificate (if applicable).** You also have to prove that you've lived together (happily or otherwise) for more than a year by supplying bills, leases, mortgage statements, love notes, monogramed towels...

★ **Bank statements.** This is Canada's way of saying, "Show me the money." Oh, and you'd better have some.

★ **Proof of education.** Secondary or postsecondary education is needed for entry. Canada doesn't need any more undereducated citizens. Newfoundland is taking care of that already. (More on that later.)

- **Your résumé.** Ask not what Canada can do for you. Show what you can do for Canada.
- **Proof of medical insurance.** Yes, Canada has nationally sponsored health care, just not for you. You're not a Canadian yet.
- **But wait, there's more!** Depending on what kind of visa you are trying to obtain, there are scores of other documents you'll need to provide. Stay organized and drink heavily through the process, and you'll be fine. More than fine. You'll be Canadian-fine.

## SPONSORED VISAS

The following sponsored visas fall under the Family Class program of Citizenship and Immigration Canada (CIC).

### KEEPING IT RELATIVE

Do you have family in Canada? Do your mom and dad run a cute little B&B in Winnipeg? Did your kid move to Vancouver to help her boyfriend run his "dispensary"? Did Grandma and Grandpa retire to a clothing-optional potato farm on Prince Edward Island? Are any of them still speaking to you? If so, then you may have just established your "in" to Canadian freedom.

According to CIC, you can obtain a visa through family sponsorship.

Of course, there are a number of requirements that must be met by your sponsoring relative in order for him or her to be eligible:

* Did your relative sponsor your Uncle Jerry and then throw him out into the snow after he got drunk and exposed himself to the neighbors on an ill-fated Boxing Day? *Not eligible or reliable.*

* Has your relative failed to make alimony or child-support payments, claiming that times are hard while clicking through channels on a new, wall-sized HD plasma television? *Not eligible and kind of an asshole.*

* Does your relative receive government assistance for any reason other than being disabled, resulting in annoyed neighbors referring to your relative, with the harshest of Canadian slang terms, as a pogey? *Not eligible and quite possibly a deadbeat.*

* Years ago, did your relative rob a Tim Hortons at gun point, claiming it was just a bad reaction to the lavender bath salts snorted earlier that day? Was it never suspended from your relative's record? *Definitely not eligible and potentially dangerous.*

- Does your relative owe money to the immigration office? *Sorry, we lost your paperwork.*
- Is your relative in prison? *Where are you supposed to stay? In the adjacent cell?*
- Is your relative in bankruptcy? *How is he or she supposed to take care of your sorry immigrant ass?*

In basic terms, your sponsor must meet income requirements that prove he or she can handle the financial burden that sponsoring you would present. Your sponsor must sign an agreement to provide food, shelter, and money to support you and whomever you convince to move with you for up to ten years, depending on your age and how you are related. Of course, you will also need to sign an agreement that states you will at least try to support yourself as a fresh-off-the-truck immigrant and submit to a medical and criminal background check. Are you feeling the love? Again, welcome to your new status as an alien.

## MY COUNTRY OR YOURS?

Have you checked out the Canadian dating websites? Perhaps a mobile app for the "desperately seeking" masses? Before swiping left, you might ask yourself if you just missed your ticket for the express train to Canadian resettlement. As an immigrant, you could participate in the age-old strategy of matrimonial relocation. This strategy, of course, is quite illegal and not recommended. (Read the warning on the following page. Seriously, read it.) If, however, you've found a Canadian conjugal candidate who makes your heart go pit-a-pat and your pants a little warmer, there are rules you and your potential spouse/sponsor would need to meet in order to be eligible.

❉ Are either of you under the age of eighteen? *Duh. Like most places, that's illegal in Canada too. Don't be a perv.*

❉ Are either of you already married to someone else? *Get real. This is Canada, not a show on TLC.*

❉ Has your spouse previously sponsored another spouse and five years haven't passed since that former spouse has become a permanent resident? *Your love-sponsor is running a scam and isn't fooling anyone.*

## What about Same-Sex Marriages?

Technically, isn't all marriage same-sex? After all, it's just the same old sex after you're married. But if you're wanting to know if Canada recognizes or allows marriage between two people of the same gender, then yes, starting in Ontario in 2003 and all other provinces and territories since 2005, same-sex marriages are recognized and allowed. Lucky for you, this increases your chances of meeting the right Canadian by 50 percent, but note that all the same rules apply.

# WARNING!

It is a crime for a foreign national to marry a Canadian citizen or permanent resident for the sole purpose of gaining entry into Canada. CIC has ways of verifying whether a marriage is real or one of "convenience." One shudders to imagine how this verification is performed, but there are some pretty stiff penalties for you and your spouse/sponsor should CIC find you in violation. So, unless you two are madly in love or really fantastic actors, don't even think about it.

## WORK VISAS

If awarding a Canadian work visa were a beauty pageant, you would be judged on your talent, your ability to intelligently express yourself, and your effectiveness in representing the values held near and dear by your fellow Canadians. If you happen to look good in a swimsuit, even better. Brazilian wax or not, priority is given to the candidates who bring a bit of razzmatazz to what is an otherwise boring and tedious process of selection. What is Canada looking for in choosing who moves on to the next round to obtaining the right to work on Canadian soil? Let's take a look, shall we?

## GOT MAD SKILLS? HERE'S YOUR WORK PERMIT!

Is there something you can do better than most Canadians? Perhaps you know how to properly prepare a meal of rabbit stuffed with elk served on a bed of barbecued beaver for a group of two hundred lumberjacks. Maybe you can create a mobile app that predicts when and where the next ice-hockey fight will break out. Do you build communication satellites in your spare time, covertly launching them from your backyard to the chagrin of your neighbors and the federal government? If this sounds like you, then you might just be the sort of skilled worker Canada is looking for.

In reviewing your application as a skilled labourer (Notice the Canadian spelling? Get used to it), you'll be judged by the following six criteria:

- **Your fluency in English or French.** Québec is a stickler for this one. If you don't speak the language, they aren't interested. They even have police to check your pronunciation. No kidding.

- **Your education.** Again, you must at least possess a high school diploma. If you have a master's degree or a PhD, move to the head of the line, smarty-pants.

- **Your work experience.** To be eligible for this program, you must have worked full-time in your profession for at least a year in the past ten years. The good news is that thirty hours a week is considered full-time in Canada.

- **Your age.** If you are in your "advanced years," how much longer do you plan to be of service to the Canadian workforce? Is this ageism? Perhaps, or maybe it's just a sign of paranoid dementia common among old farts like yourself.

- **Do you have a valid job offer?** Have you managed to convince a Canadian company that you can save the family farm and rescue the CEO's daughter from having to wear bargain brands?

- **What is the likelihood that you'll adapt and stay?** Do you show signs of being a larval-stage Canadian?

## CANADA WANTS ENTREPRENEURS! TRY THE NEW START-UP VISA

Got an idea for a business? Perhaps a posh and innovative hotel chain for the terminally ill? Bed, Breakfast, and Beyond? Know how to run it? Can you pitch it to a Canadian angel investor or venture capital fund? Can you prove that your business idea can generate at least $40,000 a year? If so, you may be in the lucky position to have provinces competing to help you gain entry with a start-up visa. After all, if putting the hospice in hospitality could increase the employment rate of a province and generate taxable revenue, why wouldn't they want you, your idea, and your potential income to help fix that traffic light in the main square that's been on the fritz since 1974? All the same documents previously mentioned will be needed as well as proof that you can handle your personal finances until your business starts buzzing.

## REFUGEE VISAS

You're worried, of course, about how the tides are continually changing in the States. You're worried about the value of the dollar, and with each new passing legislation, you see your personal freedoms slipping away one paid-for vote at a time. You find yourself standing in line at the Walmart layaway desk, reminiscing about how great your country once was, and then it hits you—I'll just show up on Canada's doorstep, tell them of my oppression, my pain, my endless inconveniences, and they, wiping tears from their eyes, will welcome me with open and sympathetic arms. I will claw my way to a new freedom, a better freedom, a freedom I am entitled to as a long-suffering American refugee. Spielberg might even make a movie about my personal struggles. I bet I'd make a bundle off of the book rights.

## WAKE THE HELL UP!

Have your neighbors been rounded up and tortured because they didn't take down their Christmas decorations after January 6? Was your spouse abducted by armed militants as a result of how you voted in the last school board election? Did you lose an arm because the local police force found out you belong to a politically suspect quilting bee?

Thought not.

*You are not a refugee. You are a drama queen.*

And in Canada, queens are on money, on playing cards, and in a few choice drag bars, where they belong.

## WHAT ABOUT POLITICAL ASYLUM?

Puh-lease! Unless you can prove that you are escaping persecution as a result of your race, caste, nationality, religion, political opinions, or membership and/or participation in a particular social group or activity, then you need to buy a ladder and get over your special brand of crazy.

Entry for refugees and those seeking political asylum is reserved for those unfortunates who face serious if not deadly consequences to themselves or their families if they stay in their country of origin. It's not for whiny poo-poo babies who think they are entitled to cheaper gas prices.

## STUDENT VISAS

If you're just not sure if Canada is the right fit for your footloose and freewheeling lifestyle, you could develop your taste for maple syrup and bitter winters by studying among other Canadians. If you plan on hitting the books for more than six months, you will probably need to complete the following to obtain a student visa:

✳ You must be accepted by a Canadian school. You're smart enough, right?

- You must prove you have money to cover tuition, living expenses, and travel for your return trip to the States. Remember, you're a student and this agreement is temporary.

- You have to agree to abide by Canadian laws and not risk national security. This is Canada's way of saying, "If you're under my roof, you're going to obey my rules!" No shenanigans and only a minimal amount of hanky-panky, please.

- You must be in good health and may even be required to submit to a medical examination. Welcome to Canada. Bend over. You may feel a little prick.

- You must convince the immigration office that you will leave when your studies are done. No, it doesn't count if you cross your fingers behind your back. Nice try.

If this seems like a dead end, remember, as a student you have the opportunity to meet lots of other Canadians. You could meet potential employers or even fall in love, paving the way toward becoming a permanent resident. If you're charming, smart, and able to adapt, this might be the ticket to your Canadian dream.

## STUDENT WORK PERMIT

So, you're a student in one of the fine Canadian institutions of learning. Perhaps you even have your spouse and/or kids in tow. What are you going to do to make money? Are you going to have to seek covert employment, getting paid under the table by unscrupulous Canadian shopkeeps who reimburse your sweat labour (there it is again) with a mere fraction of the Canadian minimum wage? Are you going to have to rent out your children to unregulated medical experiments in order to pay next month's rent? Is your spouse going to have to contribute to the household revenue by selling thousands of hand-knitted toaster-cozies on Etsy?

Fret not. If you plan on studying for more than six months to earn a diploma or professional certificate, you and your family have the opportunity to apply for a student work permit through CIC. It is only valid for the length of your studies up to a maximum of three years, but after that, you can always apply for a postgraduation work permit, which will set you on the path toward obtaining that coveted PR card.

Not a bad deal, eh? (Yeah. Get used to hearing *eh?* It really is a Canadian thing. But more aboot that later.)

# MONEY TALKS

Are you ridiculously and/or fabulously wealthy? Are you part of that notorious 1 percent who'll eventually be chased to Canada by hordes of angry hipsters holding pitchforks and zero-emission torches? Well, my capricious little capitalist, Canada can't wait to get into your pants. More specifically, the back area— y'know, the place where you keep your wallet.

If you can prove you have a net worth of at least CAN$10 million (CAD) and are willing to invest $2 million of that in the Immigrant Investor Venture Capital (IIVC) Fund, then you are just the golden calf worthy of Canadian adoration. Sure, you'll have to comply with all the same rules and provide all the same documents as the lowly peasant immigrants: language tests, medical exams, criminal records, etc., but you are rich, and you know the grading curve is in your favour (There's that extra *u* again). Canada welcomes you, your accounts, and your generous at-risk investment with a hearty handshake and possibly an open-mouth kiss. By the way, you can't live in Québec. They're not impressed, ever, and can't be so easily bought. You'll quickly learn that many Canadian rules don't apply to Québec. They're kind of a royal pain in the Canadian derriere.

Of course, if you're that wealthy, why not simply buy an island in the Caribbean? There're probably a lot of them for sale. But hey, it's your dollar. By the way, my *Guide for Buying a Tropical Island* is pending. Order your advanced copy today!

## (NOT RECOMMENDED)

## BE AN ILLEGAL ALIEN

If your spirit animal happens to be a three-toed sloth and all of this application-with-the-proper-authorities mumbo jumbo seems like a lot of effort, you could always just do it—cross the border and try to blend in. It's not like there's a big wall to jump over or endless masses of armed Canadian guards protecting the borders, but you'd better have some serious cojones. If caught, you can expect to pay substantial fines and be imprisoned up to six months. If you are a repeat offender, you could spend up to two years in a detention center. At the end of your imprisonment, you could be deported, which could very well mean they drop you off in northern Montana. Have you ever tried to hitchhike in northern Montana? It won't go well.

In addition to the possibility of being caught by the authorities, you could find yourself working under slave-like conditions for a Canadian overseer who will claim to the media that employing illegal aliens is a victimless crime while you enjoy your daily ration of stale bread and flat Diet Pepsi.

You're smarter than that. Don't do it.

## A VISA-DATA WORD SEARCH

Locate all the information you'll need to apply for your visa! Specifically, be on the lookout for puzzlers like your name, address, birthdate, citizenship, criminal record, finances, health history, income, occupation, passport, and OF COURSE, visa!

```
Y  K  D  J  D  E  Q  M  E  O  G  P  D  F
R  H  N  J  R  G  I  Y  M  T  I  I  J  S
O  F  Q  B  O  O  T  H  A  B  E  H  U  X
T  A  N  R  C  A  T  I  Y  I  M  S  Y  U
S  I  C  T  E  Z  O  M  V  R  O  N  Q  L
I  J  O  U  R  V  A  C  B  T  C  E  O  O
H  A  B  W  L  I  M  B  U  H  N  Z  A  F
H  Z  S  P  A  S  K  K  P  D  I  I  G  R
T  K  E  Z  N  A  Q  S  A  A  L  T  S  N
L  P  C  R  I  Q  W  M  Y  T  O  I  E  O
A  M  N  T  M  L  V  D  X  E  R  C  Y  I
E  L  A  K  I  M  Y  S  L  M  N  Q  B  T
H  D  N  W  R  A  W  S  S  H  H  F  V  A
Q  X  I  F  C  R  Y  Q  U  L  P  U  X  P
V  O  F  T  R  O  P  S  S  A  P  I  I  U
W  T  J  B  A  K  D  H  J  I  G  N  W  C
N  H  X  U  X  O  H  V  K  A  R  L  H  C
A  D  D  R  E  S  S  K  F  W  A  P  E  O
M  A  G  P  K  B  J  K  O  Q  S  M  W  F
E  V  L  Z  I  G  R  X  C  S  R  L  C  U
```

| | | |
|---|---|---|
| Address | Finances | Occupation |
| Birthdate | Health history | Passport |
| Citizenship | Income | Visa |
| Criminal record | Name | |

# CHAPTER

## 2

---

# PAPERWORK IS NOT TERMINAL, BUT IT CAN FEEL THAT WAY

anada eliminated the death penalty in 1976 with its last hanging—the preferred method of Canadian execution—held in 1962. Such cruelty has no place in modern Canadian culture...except when it comes to paperwork. By this point, you probably have a good idea which visa and path for Canadian entry is right for you. Grab a pen and a dose of whatever anti-anxiety medication you've been prescribed (You're an American. You know you're taking something), and get ready to dive in.

> ## WHY THE BIG MAPLE LEAF?
>
> Since the 1890s the maple leaf has served as the unofficial symbol of Canada, but it wasn't until 1965 that the Canadian flag was officially adopted as Canada's proud symbol. Before that, Britain's Union Jack flew over Canada. Needless to say, this pissed off a lot of Quebecers. Of course, there are harder things to do.

# SHOULD YOU SEEK REPRESENTATION?

Like most Americans, when a difficult task presents itself—when you find your rain gutters are clogged with the decaying corpses of a suicidal possum family, when your Hummer's faux-leather interior is defiled with regurgitated frozen margaritas and chicken quesadillas after a bachelorette party gone horribly wrong, when your creative two-year-old expresses his inner Jackson Pollock, transforming the nursery into a fragrant and avant-garde exhibition using only the contents of his diaper—you get someone else to deal with it. Facing mounds of immigration paperwork requiring the kind of precision and accuracy that most capable Americans reserve for applying eyeliner while driving or competing at beer-pong tournaments, the logical next step is finding someone else to do it for you. CIC understands your pain and does allow representation to help you dot your i's, cross your t's, and wipe your nosey-wosey when you have a sneezy-poo.

According to CIC, "a representative is someone who provides advice, consultation, or guidance to you at any stage of the application process, or in a proceeding and, if you appoint him or her as your representative by filling out (your immigration application forms), has your permission to conduct business on your behalf with Immigration, Refugees and Citizenship Canada (IRCC) and the Canada Border Services Agency (CBSA)."

You are not obligated to use a representative, and CIC, just like your mama, promises to love all her children the same, though one of them always seems to get the bigger piece of cake and doesn't have to sleep chained in the basement.

Two types of representatives are accepted by CIC, and best of all, one of them is totally free. Your options for choosing a representative follow.

## COMPENSATED REPRESENTATIVES

Compensated representatives must be authorized representatives in order to be of any use. What I am saying here is make sure, absolutely sure, they have the right credentials. If they don't, your application will be returned, and you will then be, as they say in Japan, shit out of luck.*

## UNCOMPENSATED REPRESENTATIVES (THE FREE ONES)

THIS GROUP INCLUDES BUT IS NOT LIMITED TO

* friends and family who are accustomed to your lack of motivation and your usual high-maintenance demands;
* organizations that provide such assistance to free-loaders like yourself in order to feel good about themselves (nongovernmental) or commanded by God to help the poor or those pretending to be poor (religious); or
* consultants, lawyers, Québec notaries, and supervised students-of-law who, for some reason

---

* I've never been to Japan and cannot verify the veracity of this statement.

(probably blackmail), have decided to do something very un-lawlike and not charge a fee.

> If you decide to use a representative, you will need to complete the IMM 5476 form (Use of a Representative). You'll soon notice that all immigration forms start with IMM. Try not to drown in the sea of IMM.

## FORMS, FORMS, FORMS... THEN FEES, FEES, FEES

### FAMILY SPONSORSHIP

If you've identified a Canadian family member or spouse willing to sponsor your great escape, you'll be happy to know that a majority of the paperwork needed will have to be completed by that person, not you! Winning!

**NOTE**

All forms must be completed in English or French. If you hire a translator, you will have to provide an affidavit by the translator and a notarized copy of the original. If you are not fluent in either of these languages and aren't a refugee, good luck getting in. *No bueno.*

Here's a summary of the forms you'll encounter for family sponsorship:

❋ Application to Sponsor, Sponsorship Agreement and Undertaking (IMM 1344)—This must be signed by you and your sponsor. This form starts the process, identifies all those involved in the agreement with their contact information, and outlines the terms of sponsorship as described in Chapter 1. At the end of the online application, you'll be given a bar code that needs to be included on all future documents. Like it or not, you've been automated. Welcome to Canada, number 587037.

❋ Sponsorship Evaluation (IMM 5481)—This needs to be filled out by the sponsor. Your sponsor must agree to be evaluated to ensure he or she meets all the requirements to sponsor an immigrant. This may or may not involve a probe. Depends on who's working that day. If it's Gary, he really likes the glove.

* Statutory Declaration of Common-Law Union (IMM 5409)—This only needs to be completed by the spouse or common-law partner of the sponsor. After all, that person is going to have to put up with your sorry alien ass too.

* Sponsor Questionnaire (IMM 5540)—Must be filled out by anyone sponsoring a spouse or common-law or conjugal partner. Don't worry, there are no questions about your sex life. Of course, if you want to include some details, that might speed up the process a bit. Could also slow it down, depending on what you two are into.

## Pay Your Fee

This can be anywhere from CAN$75 to $475 depending on the relationship to the sponsor. While you're at it, you might as well pay your Right to Permanent Resident Fee (CAN$490), which is due upon approval of your application. Of course, if your application is not approved, you'll get a refund sometime before senility sets in.

## How Long Does It Take to Process This Application?

According to CIC, the current wait time varies according to the relationship with the sponsor. A dependent child can wait a year and a half, while a spouse can be kept waiting more than two years. According to the website, grandparents can take as long as five years, increasing the likelihood they'll die before getting their healthcare card. Again, in the land of government-sponsored health care, they don't want new citizens who need to go to the doctor a lot.

# THE WACKY AND WONDERFUL WORLD OF WORK VISAS

If you've decided to join the Canadian workforce, there are several paths toward permanent residency for you to choose from, each with its own unique forms and applications. For your reading displeasure, here are some of the most popular options.

### Getting Invited (a.k.a. Express Entry Visas)

This is the process applied to manage the Federal Skilled Workers Program, the Federal Skilled Trades Program, and the Canadian Experience Class. In basic terms, as an applicant for Express Entry, you've identified yourself as having a skill, a trade, and/or professional experience that would make you desirable to Canadian employers. You may have even received a job offer from a Canadian or a nomination certificate from a province or territory that wants your skills, experience, or trade within its borders. There are various levels of skill and trade, and those possessing the skills and experience most needed in Canada are given a higher score and are moved to the head of the line to be invited as a permanent resident.

To see if you are eligible for an Express Entry Visa, you should first take the online assessment through the Canadian immigration page.

Once your assessment has been completed, you may or may not receive the coveted Invitation to Apply. You'll likely receive this invitation if you

* have a valid job offer;
* have been nominated by a province or territory; or
* are among the top ranked within your pool based on skill and/or experience.

> The border between Canada and the U.S. is the world's longest unprotected border. Certain businessmen-turned-politicians shockingly don't have an opinion on this.

### Does Express Really Mean Express?

According to CIC, if the application is accurately completed and none of the i's are dotted with little hearts, the processing time can be less than six months. This is practically the speed of light by governmental standards.

### Is There a Fee If I'm Accepted?

Don't be naive. Of course there's a fee. What? Are they just going to let you in without extending the palm? As noted above, there is a CAN$490 Permanent Resident Fee. Don't be stingy, you've paid more splitting a large Diet Coke in Disneyland with your ungrateful kid.

## Start a Canadian Company—Start-Up Visas

If you have an idea for a business you'd like to start in Canada and even have an investor lined up to make it happen, then you are well on your way to Canadian business ownership. Here's a comprehensive list of the forms you may need to fill out to make this dream a reality:

* IMM 0008—Generic Application Form for Canada

- ⚜ IMM 0008 DEP—Additional Dependents/Declaration
- ⚜ IMM 5669—Schedule A: Background/Declaration
- ⚜ IMM 5562—Supplementary Information: Your Travels
- ⚜ IMM 0008 Schedule 13—Business Immigration Programs: Start-Up Business Class
- ⚜ IMM 5406—Additional Family Information
- ⚜ IMM 5476—Use of Representative (if you're using one)

You'll also need:

- ⚜ Travel documents and passports
- ⚜ Proof of language proficiency
- ⚜ Letter of support from your investor
- ⚜ Identity and all civil documents
- ⚜ Children's information (if you have 'em)
- ⚜ Police certificates and clearances
- ⚜ Photos
- ⚜ Fees and settlement funds

*Did we mention there would be paperwork?* If you're OK with reading through tear-filled eyes, let's continue.

## Artist, Athlete, or Farmer? The Canadian Triple Threat

If you'd like to gain entry into Canada as a scrappy, self-employed go-getter, there are three very distinct career paths that the Canadian government is willing to give you a shot at: as a cultural contributor, as an athlete or athletic supporter (that means a coach, smarty-pants), or as a farmer. Canada supports artists who support themselves and contribute to the cultural enrichment of Canadian citizens. Athletes are welcome to train future Olympians and hockey players. Farmers make food, and Canada loves food (more about that in future chapters). As a self-employed applicant, you are required to fill out all the forms and supply all the documents listed above for a start-up visa with the exception of a letter of support from your investor.

You will, however, need to supply the following documentation:

* **Proof of education.** All certifications, diplomas, and supporting documentation. Canada wants brains!

* **Proof of relevant experience.** Your cultural activities must be of a world-class level. No, appearing in the chorus of your high school's

production of *Brigadoon* doesn't count. Same goes for your athletic history. World-class means world-class. Winning the local Little League championship means nothing to them. Honestly, it means little to anyone. Stop telling those stories. Have you managed a farm? Bring a pitchfork to your interview and maybe wear overalls.

- **Proof of adaptability.** This is about your spouse or common-law partner's ability to find something productive to do while you're painting nudes in the basement, pumping future Olympians with "performance enhancers," or rescuing Bessie from the ravine. Your partner must provide evidence of his or her education, ability to obtain a work permit, and ties to any Canadian relatives.
- As a farmer you may have to fill out Form EIEIO... just kidding.
- All the same fees apply.

## Want to Buy Your Way In?

As noted in Chapter 1, if you have the moola, then Canada welcomes you with an awkwardly long and lingering embrace. The process of applying as an Immigrant Investor requires that one wait for the Immigrant Investor Venture Capital Pilot Program to open for applications. At the time this book was written, no further applications were being accepted, having satisfied the sixty initial investors needed, but with the inevitable collapse of the U.S. economy, Canada is sure to open up that sucker again. You're rich, you can wait. Even better, you can pay someone to wait for you.

> Canada is the largest producer of uranium in the world.

## Before You Start Work, What Is Your SIN?

No one in Canada wants to know how many times you've touched yourself in the past week. Except Russell; everyone in Canada has learned to ignore Russell. In the States, you had a Social Security number, but in Canada, you'll be trading that in for your Social Insurance Number (SIN). You'll need it to work in Canada and eventually enjoy government programs and benefits.

When you first arrive in Canada, tell the border services officer (BSO) you're there to work. If you've been given a Port of Entry (POI) Letter of Introduction (LOI) from a Canadian visa office, bring it with you. It's not a travel document or a work permit; it is simply proof of your intent to work and the government's approval for you to enter with that intent. You should also bring any other supporting documents and proof of medical insurance. If everything is in order, the BSO will print your work permit right there. Once you have your work permit and head past the border, make a beeline to the nearest Service Canada office to get your SIN.

If you have a spouse in tow, he or she will need to do the same and may be eligible for an open work permit that will allow him or her to accept any job offer from any employer while in Canada.

Read your work permit carefully. All the conditions for your employment should be detailed on it. If you are in violation of any of the conditions, you could be asked to leave Canada, and that would be embarrassing.

Again, there are other options for entry into Canada, but these are the most usual and popular methods. Explore your options carefully, and make sure your paperwork is impeccably prepared.

Best of luck in leaving the U.S. as a laborer and entering Canada as a labourer. You've earned that superfluous *u*.

# FIND YOUR VISA
# WORD SEARCH

Locate your specific brand of visa in the word search on the next page! As a recap, your options include: family, illegal, investor, marriage, political asylum, self-employed, student, refugee, and work (the most fun of all).

```
B F F S S K O R R N R C O W
P U L O M O T V K P K H U J
O P Q K Z V U O Y L I M A F
L L V G Y Z R C T N Q O L M
I U X A G K L Q C R C A M D
T J F N I K D C E V G A Q H
I I O P C M I C T E R S I L
C I N C Z S J N L R Q E W F
A O D V P X E L I R L L D Q
L Q X Y E D I A P K K F L O
A W Y K U S G V E J Y E A N
S X N T F E T T D W M M R E
Y W S Q S N S O N O F P E F
L M O R G J P N R O V L F E
U P V R F I E B K S H O U Z
M B I L K M L E U G F Y G W
U J B W I W R N P X N E E G
E A V W Y K F S F W W D E Z
M P V Z O E M B H H R W J D
R G N O Q L V U M Y H I E H
```

Family                    Refugee
Illegal                   Self-employed
Investor                  Student
Marriage                  Work
Political asylum

# 3

# LEARNING HOW TO SPEAK LIKE A CANUK (WHICH MEANS CANADIAN)

ongratulations! You've chosen your path for Canadian entry, gathered all your documents, filled out and turned in all your paperwork—now all you have to do is wait. A response from CIC could take up to six months, and obtaining your visa, if it is approved, could take even longer. Americans are not known for their patience, but you are becoming a Canadian. Use this opportunity to exercise the kind of patience that helps the average Canuck make it through what feels like a lifetime of winter. Find ways to fill the time. Practice deep breathing, maybe look into past-lives transgression therapy, or, even better, learn the Canadian lingo while you're lingering in limbo.

As stated repeatedly, there are two official languages of Canada—English and French—but since it's been established that Québec wants little to do with you, we'll focus on English. Besides, as a Yank, you are probably what Canadians would call an anglophone—one who only speaks English. To help you wrap your mouth around the Canadian tongue, and you know you want to, try reading the following story. Pay close attention to the under-lined words and phrases; there's going to be a quiz afterward.

I awoke to the sound of the <u>garburator</u> and grabbed my <u>housecoat</u>, slipping on my ratty <u>thongs</u> and a fresh <u>gitch</u>. My roomie Ian was making a <u>kerfuffle</u> around the <u>chesterfield</u>, picking up what was left of the <u>two-four</u> and that empty <u>mickey</u> we polished off before <u>head'r</u> to the <u>booze can</u> down in <u>Van</u> where the guitarist for <u>Barenaked Ladies</u> was really <u>giv'n her</u> for his bud's <u>stag</u>. Rubbing my <u>Molson muscle</u> and craving a <u>double-double</u> and a <u>BeaverTail</u>, I grabbed my <u>toque</u> and my <u>runners</u>, brushed my teeth over the rusty <u>tap</u> in the <u>washroom</u>, threw on some <u>track pants</u>, grabbed my <u>knapsack</u>, and <u>head'r</u> out with a pocketful of <u>loonies</u> and <u>toonies</u>.

That <u>chinook</u> the <u>humidex</u> predicted had arrived, bringing in one <u>skookum</u> of a storm. With that much lightning, I hoped the <u>hydro</u> wouldn't get <u>hooped</u>. After splashing through a half a <u>click</u> of puddles from the neighborhood's faulty <u>eavestroughs</u>, my <u>runners</u> were transformed into <u>soakers</u>. I entered the <u>GT Boutique</u> and removed my drenched <u>toque</u>. Ian's friend Gary was working behind the counter with his goofy grin.

"How's it goin', <u>eh?</u>" he waved. He's such a <u>keener</u> when he's not being a total <u>hoser</u>. Ian and I had invited him out on a road trip to <u>Gastown</u> but dumped him when we found out he didn't drink anything stronger than <u>pop</u>, didn't eat anything spicier than <u>pablum</u>, and really enjoyed <u>five-pin bowling</u>. Gary never made it past <u>public school</u> and helped out at the market when he wasn't working at <u>Rotten Ronnies</u>. His manager at <u>McDicks</u> thought he was the densest <u>Newfie</u> in the <u>postal code</u>. Well, at least he was working and not on the <u>pogey.</u>

"What can I <u>fetch'er?</u>" he asked.

"Just a <u>double-double</u> and a <u>BeaverTail</u>," I replied.

"<u>Fer'sure</u>. Oh, we're all outta <u>homo</u>. Is <u>whitener</u>

OK?" he asked while grabbing a pastry out of the case with a fresh serviette.

"Nah, I hate whitener. I'll just buy some milk in a bag," I called out, heading to the dairy section. On my way, a Girl Guide grabbed my attention, asking if I'd like to buy a chocolate bar to help her get her entrepreneurship badge.

"What kinds of chocolate bars are you selling?" I asked. Opening her box, I could see she had Smarties, Caramilk, Crispy Crunch, Coffee Crisp, and even a homemade Nanaimo bar. At a twoonie a piece, it seemed like a bargain. While I was distracted, the girl's mom snatched up the last of the milk. The little bugger totally deked me out.

Returning to the queue, I could tell that the snowbirds had returned with the spring, adding substantially to the lineup. I was tempted to wrap a pop and a small box of Shreddies in an elastic under my jacket and head out the door, if it weren't for the Mountie sitting on his arse in the Muskoka chair by the entrance.

# WHAT DID I JUST READ?

Lost? Well, study up! Here are the definitions of all of the common Canadian terms that you just read about—hopefully you were able to use context clues to define most of them!

## ORGANIZED IN STORY ORDER:

- **garburator**—garbage disposal
- **housecoat**—bathrobe
- **thongs**—flip-flops
- **gitch/gotch/gaunch/gonch/ginch/gotchies/gitchies/gonchies**—men's underwear (BTW, wedgies are called gotchie-pulls)
- **kerfuffle**—commotion or fuss
- **chesterfield**—couch
- **two-four**—case of twenty-four beers (roughly enough for two Canadians)
- **mickey**—small bottle of booze, usually 375 milliliters [not to be confused with a twenty-sixer (750 milliliters) or a forty-pounder (1.14 liters)]
- **head'r**—slang for the act of departing
- **booze can**—after-hours and usually illegal bar or tavern
- **Van**—short for *Vancouver*

- **Barenaked Ladies**—Canadian band that actually made it big in the States
- **giv'n her**—giving 100 percent
- **stag/stagette**—bachelor or bachelorette party
- **Molson muscle**—beer belly
- **double-double**—coffee with two creams and two sugars
- **BeaverTail**—Canadian pastry of fried dough with sweet toppings
- **toque/tuque**—knit cap
- **runners**—athletic shoes
- **tap**—spigot
- **washroom**—bathroom or restroom
- **track pants**—sweatpants
- **knapsack**—backpack

### CANADIAN BACON

If you've ever been to France, you know they don't serve french fries, and in Canada, Canadian bacon is simply called back bacon or, more specifically, peameal bacon. Don't sound like a hoser gorby when ordering breakfast.

- **loonie**—Canadian $1 coin (named for the loon featured on the coin)

- **toonie or twoonie**—Canadian $2 coin (play on the word *loonie*)
- **chinook**—a warm wind
- **humidex**—much like the heat index in the States; calculation based on heat and humidity
- **skookum**—great or powerful
- **hydro**—electric utilities
- **hooped**—broken
- **click or klick**—a kilometer
- **eavestrough**—rain gutter
- **soaker or booter**—drenched shoes
- **GT Boutique**—slang for Giant Tiger stores
- **eh?**—common expression that beckons agreement
- **keener**—brownnoser
- **hoser**—idiot
- **Gastown**—oldest neighborhood and tourist trap in Vancouver
- **pop**—soda
- **pablum**—baby food
- **five-pin bowling**—like regular bowling but with five pins and a smaller ball (an excuse to drink beer)
- **public school**—elementary school

> ## IS HOCKEY THE NATIONAL SPORT?
> Yes, it's the official winter sport, but lacrosse is the official summer one. Oh, and basketball was invented by Canadian phys ed teacher James Naismith.

- **Rotten Ronnies or McDicks**—McDonald's
- **Newfie**—derogatory term for those from Newfoundland
- **postal code**—zip code
- **pogey or on the pogey**—someone receiving government assistance
- **fetch'er**—get for you
- **Fer'sure**—absolutely
- **homo**—whole milk (try not to giggle)
- **whitener**—nondairy creamer, usually powdered
- **serviette**—napkin
- **milk in a bag**—usually sold in sets of three totaling 4 liters
- **Girl Guide**—Girl Scout
- **chocolate bar**—candy bar
- **Smarties, Caramilk, Crispy Crunch, Coffee Crisp**—popular Canadian candies
- **Nanaimo bar**—popular no-bake chocolate, custard, and crushed wafer Canadian dessert

- **deke or being deked out**—outmaneuvered. Short for *decoy* and usually used for athletics, particularly hockey, but can be used for real-world situations too.
- **queue or lineup**—any line for waiting
- **snowbirds**—those who seasonally relocate to avoid the winter cold
- **Shreddies**—popular Canadian cereal
- **elastic**—rubber band
- **Mountie**—officer in the Royal Canadian Mounted Police (RCMP)
- **arse**—ass or butt. Can also be called a bum.
- **Muskoka chair**—Adirondack chair

## SPECIAL WORDS AND PHRASES FOR STUDENTS

If you are entering Canada with a student visa, the following words and phrases might come in handy:

- **write a test**—to take a test or exam
- **invigilate**—to proctor an examination
- **mark a test**—to grade a test
- **tutorial**—to offer a recitation or present to a very small class

- **supply teacher**—substitute teacher
- **college**—any community-based college (not to be confused with a university)
- **public school**—elementary school
- **zed**—*Z*, last letter in the alphabet
- **rye & ginger**—popular Canadian cocktail/study aid: Canadian whiskey and ginger ale (Canada Dry, of course)

### WHAT'S A ROBERTSON SCREW?

Don't get excited, students. This isn't a drink. Robertson screws and screwdrivers have a square head and are nearly impossible to strip, unlike the Phillips-head screws of the U.S. They would've become popular in the States if Henry Ford didn't demand exclusive rights and Robertson refused to sell.

## WHEN DINING OUT

- Ask for the bill, not the check.
- Ask for ketchup chips if you want fries; otherwise expect them to be served with mayo.
- Learn to love poutine. It's easy to love. French

fries covered in brown gravy and melted cheese curd. Canadian heaven.

- Brown bread is wheat bread.
- Back bacon is Canadian bacon.
- "All dressed" can be used for pizza, chips, and hot dogs. It usually means "with everything."
- When ordering a Molson, just say, "Gimme a Canadian."
- Icing sugar is powdered sugar.
- Processed cheese is American cheese, and don't order it. It's gross.
- It's not a parking garage, it's a parkade.
- Don't order a gyro, order a donair.
- Pecan pie is a butter tart minus the pecans.
- Biffy can be used to refer to any washroom.
- Tourtieres are delicious meat pies.
- Wipe your mouth with a serviette, not a napkin.
- Tim Hortons is sacred and even has its own Visa credit card.
- Tip your server. This is Canada, not Europe.

**WHAT DOES THE CANADIAN MOTTO MEAN?**

*A Mari usque ad Mare* is Canada's Latin motto, which means from sea to sea, which seems more like an obvious observation than a motto.

# INAPPROPRIATE CANADIAN TERMS YOU SHOULD NEVER USE (BUT ARE JUST FUN TO KNOW)

* **beaver**—a woman's nether region. Not to be confused with a BeaverTail, which is a pastry, although both are better when warmed a bit.
* **"Bieber my balls"**—ambiguous expression that can creep into almost any situation. Belieber or not, don't be tempted to use it.
* **bittie**—easy girl or elderly woman. Either way, don't use it.
* **bumblefuck**—nowhere, the boonies
* **cancer cage**—designated smoking area
* **Canucklehead**—derogatory name for fans of the Vancouver Canucks Hockey Club

- **cockknocker**—jerk
- **deego**—gram of marijuana
- **doo-doo head**—idiot
- **fuck the dog**—to do nothing
- **fuddle-duddle**—to fuck off
- **Gorby**—Great Outdoors Recreational Bastard; derogatory term for tourists
- **gunt**—the area between the navel and the beaver. Highly inappropriate. Never punch anyone in the gunt.

> When a Canadian says he's making a run south of the border, where do you think he's heading? Clue: It ain't Mexico.

- **Gynecology Row**—first row of seats in a strip club
- **Hongcouver**—derogatory name for Vancouver due to the amount of Asians living there. Only assholes use this term. Don't be an asshole.
- **horse cocks**—pickled sausages sold at bars. May cause one to "hork" (vomit).
- **lard ace**—fat person. Just mean and not very Canadian-like.
- **loser cruiser**—public bus
- **Newfie**—derogatory term for people from

Newfoundland and Labrador. You'll hear a lot of "Newfie" jokes, just don't tell them to any Newfies. Not unless you want to explain them and then get beat up.

* **panty remover**—gin
* **prairie dog**—needing to really have a bowel movement (its head is peeking out)
* **rock a piss**—to pee outdoors
* **rock the canoe**—to have sex
* **suckhole**—Goody Two-shoes
* **thunderbox**—not-so-delicate term for washroom

So, now you should have a grasp on some of the subtle and not-so-subtle nuances of Canadian colloquialisms. Try them out on your friends and family. They may find them amusing, or they may schedule you for some involuntary rest at a behavioral health clinic. Either way, you are becoming the Canadian you were always meant to be.

Canada's national animals are the beaver and the Canadian horse.

# MATCH THE WORDS WITH THEIR DEFINITIONS

**eecdfhrtiesl**

couch

**eyickm**

small bottle of booze

**neoiot**

Canadian $2 coin

**tienuom**

officer in the Royal Canadian Mounted Police (RCMP)

**vesrteeit**

napkin

**ueatoshoc**

bathrobe

**raedakenb dsilae**

Canadian band that actually made it big in the States

**atgs/geettast**

bachelor/bachelorette party

**rlig edigu**

Girl Scout

**esar**

ass or butt

**ANSWER:**

# 4

# CREATING CANADIAN PRIDE

nowing Canada's lingo is a great first step in learning to become a Canadian, but for you to be properly Canadianized, you must understand what is at the heart of your fellow Canucks, what makes them tick. This chapter will focus on the nuances that really set Canadians apart from the Yanks and what you'll need to know to assimilate into the maple-leaf culture. Think of it as Canadian camouflage for your soul. Fake it till you make it, right?

# GOVERNMENT

Ah, the exact thing you are running from in America… but is it really better in the Great White North?

> The Canadian National Anthem, "O Canada," though composed in 1880, was not adopted as the official anthem until a hundred years later.

The answer is yes. Plus far more whimsical.

Let's start with this comforting fact: they don't have a president. They have too much Europe in them for that. They even recognize the Queen of England, but somehow she is Queen of Canada to them(?).

They also have a prime minister. How magical does that sound? Canada is essentially like Hogwarts and to us mudblood Americans, we have a *lot* to learn. Here is a graph to try to teach you the ins and outs! It is still pretty confusing, though, so at the very least, you have some buzzwords to play with.

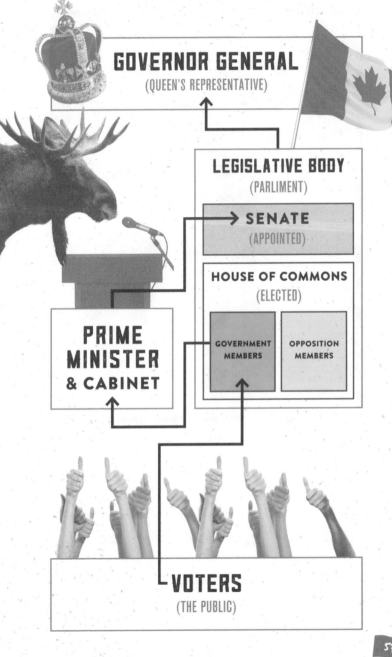

**GOVERNOR GENERAL**
(QUEEN'S REPRESENTATIVE)

**LEGISLATIVE BODY**
(PARLIMENT)

**SENATE**
(APPOINTED)

**HOUSE OF COMMONS**
(ELECTED)

GOVERNMENT MEMBERS

OPPOSITION MEMBERS

**PRIME MINISTER & CABINET**

**VOTERS**
(THE PUBLIC)

2015's newly elected Canadian Prime Minister Justin Trudeau rides moose, threatening Vladimir Putin and all foreign leaders.

# WEIGHTS AND MEASURES

Canada's government officially started the process of metrication (yes, that's a word) in 1971 with the creation of the Metric Commission. By 1977, all road signs had been converted from the imperial measurement of miles to metric kilometers. Over the years, other units of measure have slowly converted to the metric system, requiring the entire country to not only accept but actually understand how the metric system works. Rainfall is measured in millimeters, while snow is measured in centimeters. Fahrenheit switched over to Celsius in 1975, causing pot roasts to burn throughout the provinces. This conversion presented a number of challenges to Canadians, and poor training in metrication resulted in a near-tragic accident in 1983 when an Air Canada flight ran out of fuel and was forced into a glide landing on a racetrack.

Canadians buy gas in liters and obey speed limits set in kilometers per hour (km/h). Odometers and speedometers are metric, though many vehicles may have an auxiliary display for miles per hour (mph). There are some remnants of the imperial units of measure, though. Most Canadians will announce their weight or height in pounds, feet, and inches, although their licenses will list them in metric units. Most Canadian kitchens rely on Fahrenheit along with the usual imperial cooking measurements (i.e., cups, tablespoons, teaspoons, etc.). Many Canadians will use both imperial and metric measurements in daily conversation, switching between acres and hectares, ounces and grams, feet and meters, which will, no doubt, leave you hating math more than you probably already do.

Here is a little brush-up on the metric system. Read it. Memorize it. Learn to love it.

The international system of units (SI) consists of seven base units for measurement.

| ABBREVIATION | UNIT | MEASURES... |
|---|---|---|
| m | meter | length |
| kg | kilogram | mass |
| s | second | time |
| A | ampere | electric current |
| K | Kelvin | thermodynamic temperature |
| mol | mole | amount of substance |
| cd | candela | luminous intensity |

For the purposes of this book, however, we're going to stick to the basics, the day-to-day measurements you'd encounter on a simple trip to the Giant Tiger to pick up a liter of milk.

If you've had some schooling in the metric system, you'd remember to keep in mind that it is a system based off of the number ten. If you have ten fingers, you can figure out the metric system. If you have fewer than ten fingers, you'll have to improvise. If you have more, I'd like to see photos.

## LENGTH AND DISTANCE

A meter is a little more than a yard, and a kilometer (1,000 meters) is a little over half a mile. Because reasons.

| STANDARD | METRIC | OR... |
| --- | --- | --- |
| 1 inch | 2.54 centimeters | 25.4 millimeters |
| 1 foot | 0.3048 meter | 30.48 centimeters |
| 1 yard | 0.9144 meter | |
| 1 mile | 1.609 kilometers | 5,280 feet |
| 0.6214 mile | 1 kilometer | 1,000 meters |
| 3.28 feet | 1 meter | |
| 0.3937 inch | 1 centimeter | 10 millimeters |
| 0.039 inch | 1 millimeter | 0.1 centimeter |

Canada has more donut shops per capita than the U.S.

## VOLUME

A liter is the volume of a cube with 10-centimeter sides. It is a little over a quart, and a U.S. gallon is a little under 4 liters. This is handy for both shopping and cooking but perhaps useless across the board as none of these conversions are clean and therefore what you used to do in the States is now useless.

> Canada has 9 percent of the world's renewable water supply and 10 percent of the world's forests.

| STANDARD | METRIC |
| --- | --- |
| 1.06 quarts | 1 liter |
| 0.03 fluid ounce | 1 milliliter |
| 1 fluid ounce | 29.57 milliliters |
| 1 U.S. gallon | 3.785 liters |
| 1 imperial gallon | 4.546 liters |

## WEIGHT

For those of you considering moving to British Columbia, you'll find this information about grams and milligrams quite helpful, but more about that later.

| STANDARD | METRIC |
| --- | --- |
| 1 pound | 0.45 kilogram |
| 1 ounce | 28.35 grams |
| 1 ton | 907.18 kilograms |
| 0.04 ounce | 1 gram |
| 0.000035 ounce | 1 milligram |

Canada consumes more Kraft Macaroni & Cheese and fruit juice than any other nation.

With a bit of self-assured perseverance and American determination, you can quickly unlock the mystery of Canada's metric system while enjoying liters upon liters of Molson and munching grams and grams of ketchup chips and horse cocks (see previous chapter).

## CO-EXISTING IN CO-CANADA

From the ancient Latin prefix for "together, mutually, or jointly," the prefix co- will soon become part of your daily life in Canada. There is co-operation among its people, many of whom belong to various co-ops within their co-mmunities. They work together as a co-llective, often serving on co-mmissions where they co-llaborate and try to form a co-nsensus to co-exist in a co-habitive environment that promotes a co-mingling of ideas and perspectives. This may not sit well with the individ-ualistic nature of most U.S. citizens, but it is a fact of life and a source of pride among the Canucks...except Québec. Get used to the phrase "except Québec."

The values that define most Canadians are tied to their historic role as a peacekeeping and polite—almost too polite—nation. Seriously, if you ever accidentally bump into a Canadian, he or she will apologize for your rudeness and maybe even buy you coffee.

Equality, freedom, peace, and law and order are the pillars of Canadian society. Everyone has the right to speak out, though few ever do (except in Québec). Differences are greeted with acceptance throughout Canada (except in Québec). Everyone is treated with respect and dignity (unless they're in Québec).

Nonviolence is a way of life, and peace is valued above all else. (This is actually true in Québec too. They may be a pain in the arse, but they are no less Canadian.)

Its citizens may have their share of problems and disagree from time to time, but Canada is a nation bound together by simple values and genuine respect for its citizens. This is probably the result of winter trying to wipe them all out each year.

# SPENDING IN CANADA

COMMON DENOMINATIONS OF CANADIAN CURRENCY ARE AS FOLLOWS:

## COINS:

Penny 1¢ (Being phased out of circulation since 2012. Prices are rounded up to the nearest .05.)

Nickel 5¢

Dime 10¢

Quarter 25¢

Half-Dollar or Half Loonie 50¢

One-Dollar or Loonie $1

Two-Dollar or Twoonie or Toonie $2

## BANKNOTES:

$5

$10

$20

$50

$100

> ## FUN FACT
>
> After the death of Canadian actor Leonard Nimoy, fans took to "Spocking fivers." The gag was to sketch over the image of former Prime Minister Wilfrid Laurier, transforming the former head of state into the Vulcan Science Officer Mr. Spock. The Canadian mint has since changed the design of its $5 banknote to prevent such antics. Buzzkills.

## WORK VERSUS LIFE

With ten days per year of mandatory paid vacation for full-time employees, Canada is more generous than the U.S., which requires no paid vacation from employers, although many offer this benefit to their employees to avoid having their offices burned to the ground. In addition, there are five paid national holidays, referred to as statutory holidays in Canada. They are New Year's Day (January 1), Good Friday (Friday before Easter), Canada Day (July 1), Labour Day (first Monday in September), and Christmas Day (December 25).

Federal employees also observe the following: Easter Monday (in lieu of Good Friday, Monday after Easter Day), Victoria Day (Monday on or before May 24), Thanksgiving (second Monday in October),

Remembrance Day (November 11), and Boxing Day (December 26).

Depending on what province or territory you end up in, there are a number of other paid holidays you may enjoy from Armistice Day in Newfoundland and Labrador to Terry Fox Day* in Manitoba.

## WHO IS TERRY FOX?*

This athlete-turned-activist was born in 1958 in Winnipeg, Manitoba. After losing his leg to cancer, he embarked on a cross-Canada run in 1980 to raise awareness for cancer research. Unfortunately, his cancer spread and he ended his run after 143 days and 3,339 miles. He lost his battle with cancer in 1981 but won the war for cancer research. He is a true national hero and an eternal inspiration to every young Canadian.

With a surplus of days off and a culture that works to live, not lives to work, you may find yourself settling into a form of relaxation unfamiliar to most Americans. It's called a healthy work/life balance. You'll adjust and hopefully use that time to get to know those strangers that live with you. You know, those people everyone calls your spouse and kids.

## WHAT NOT TO DO IN CANADA

As we get older, we learn to separate fact from fiction. Taxes are real while extra legroom in coach is fiction. Manson is disturbingly real while the Tooth Fairy is disturbingly fiction. No, Virginia, there is no Santa Claus, but there really is a Department of Homeland Security. As adults, we learn to separate these two categories, which is why the peace-loving and polite Canucks go bat-shit crazy, and rightfully so, when a dumbass American refers to Canada as not being a real country and says that its economy is solely based on the export of maple syrup and Céline Dion. Don't be that guy. Don't even pretend to be related to that guy. If you want to live peacefully among the Canadians, you will not make this kind of stupid mistake.

*That said, maple syrup and Céline Dion are kind of important.*

Americans are a proud people, and so are Canadians, in a barely detectable way. Bragging about the price of your car, the amount of your salary, the size of your new wife's bosom, or your kid's honor roll status in pre-K might play well at your high school reunion, but not so much in Canada. It's being boastful, which is considered vulgar among Canadians. Canucks rarely share their pride verbally, unless, of course, they're discussing hockey. Then all bets are off.

> The average life-span of a Canadian is 81.16, the sixth highest in the world. Don't ask where the U.S. ranked. It's not good.

Insult a Canadian's mom, his kids, his hair, his home, but God help you if you insult his hockey team. First of all, never refer to the game as "ice hockey." In Canada, it is simply called hockey, and it is a religion, not a pastime. Female groupies refer to themselves as puck bunnies, and some fans have been known to be buried wearing their team's jersey. If loving hockey is a Canadian stereotype, it still doesn't do Canadians' love of the game justice. Like a Kardashian's sex life, the sport is a combination of incredible grace and horrific violence. It is a tribute to winter survival with places of honor bestowed upon such notable players as "The Great One," Wayne Gretzky.

> Canada's literacy rate is more than 99 percent. Again, don't ask where the U.S. ranked. It's embarrassing.

Canadians have a proud history of stepping up to support peace missions throughout the world, joining World War II on September 3, 1939, by declaring war on Germany two years before the U.S. made its declaration. Canadians have a military, and they have an arsenal of weapons. Canadian citizens have guns, but they don't go whack-a-doodle about their gun rights. They don't have open-carry laws, nor do they want them. Remember one of the pillars of their society is peace? As Americans, perhaps we've become desensitized to the amount of gun violence in our own country, a problem our Canadian neighbors are concerned about. Keeping that kind of crazy outside its borders is important to Canada and its citizens. Railing on about the Second Amendment and your right to own and carry multiple big-ass guns will not win you many Canadian friends.

Sadly, gun violence still plays a part in Canadian life. They've had their share of school shootings and random drive-bys too. But unlike their American cousins, Canadians do not use these incidents to debate the virtue of guns but rather acknowledge the sad and senseless nature of freedom misused and the violation of Canada's treasured peace. If you are tempted to assert your opinion that more and bigger guns are the answer, you will find yourself drinking your two-four of Labatt alone.

# COLOR THE FAMOUS CANADIANS

Illustrate the illustrious stars from up north!

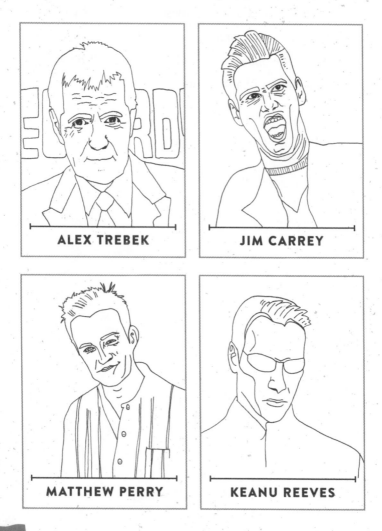

**ALEX TREBEK**

**JIM CARREY**

**MATTHEW PERRY**

**KEANU REEVES**

**CÉLINE DION**

**MICHAEL BUBLÉ**

**PAMELA ANDERSON**

HEY
GIRL

**RYAN GOSLING**

**SHANIA TWAIN**

**WILLIAM SHATNER**

**AVRIL LAVIGNE**

**JUSTIN BIEBER**

# BUT WHAT IS HABITABLE IN CANADA?

hile your visa application is being processed, you can devote a bit of time deciding just what part of Canada is right for you. In the good ol' USA you had fifty different states that offered a variety of climates, scenery, and culture to choose from, each with its very own themed Applebee's.

Lucky for you, your new homeland of frost and maple has ten different provinces and three adventure-filled territories for you to choose from, all united in surviving the soul-crushing Canadian winter.

Need help deciding which regional gem is the perfect fit in your pursuit of the Canadian dream? Here's a handy little list for your consideration.

# THE CANADIAN PROVINCES

## ALBERTA (AB)

**POPULATION**–4,121,700

**CAPITAL**–Edmonton

**LARGEST CITY**–Calgary

**OFFICIAL LANGUAGE**–English

A.K.A. the Wild Rose Province, the Princess Province, the Energy Province, the Sunshine Province. Surprisingly, no one calls it Fat Albert or Weird Al.

If you're one of the thousands of true patriots who participate in the great American tradition of citizen-based, freedom militias, congratulations, your hobby of doomsday prepping is about to pay off. Assuming you live in Montana (and what angry militant worth his salt doesn't?), why not pack up the ATV with your ACRs, RPDs, MREs, and as many other menacing acronyms that'll fit? Don't forget the kids as you and your assortment of wives head due north toward a different freedom, an authentic freedom, an Albertan freedom.

Taking advantage of the affordable real-estate market, you'll soon be enjoying your little compound on the prairie, nestled in the strategic flatlands of Alberta. Just imagine how secure you and your family will feel when you can literally watch your enemy approach for days.

If the coast is clear and you're not a fundamentalist Christian, grab a shovel and head out to Dinosaur Provincial Park, one of the richest dinosaur fossil deposits in the world and one of the few Albertan attractions not named after Winston Churchill. On second thought, even if you are a hardened and unflappable creationist, go anyway. Get some sun. It's a great place to hold a sign and shout at your fellow Albertans. Don't expect them to shout back, though. It's just not a very Albertan thing to do.

> The Trans-Canada Highway is the longest in the world at 7,821 kilometers, or 4,860 miles.

## BRITISH COLUMBIA (BC)

**POPULATION**—4,631,300

**CAPITAL**—Victoria

**LARGEST CITY—Vancouver**

**OFFICIAL LANGUAGE—English**

**A.K.A.** Beautiful British Columbia, the Pacific Province, British California, the Wet Coast. Do not call it Hippieland, Weedsville, or Potsylvania, no matter how much you're tempted.

If your inner-West-Coast-liberal has a hankering for a $6 free-trade, Arabica bean, cold-pour, dark roast with a blunt the size of an eco-friendly kombucha bottle on the side, perhaps British Columbia is the province for you.

If you consider yourself one of the millions of bohemian individualists occupying California, Oregon, or Washington, fill your native-inspired, hemp-constructed satchel with organic probiotic snacks, hop in your co-oped Tesla, and set your GPS for north. If you're one of the three liberals in Alaska, head south. Your neighbors will probably throw you a parade as you leave.

Once in BC, you'll stand in awe of the province's amazing Pacific beauty, naturally enhanced by your choice of legal narcotics. For a mere $400,000 you can afford a cozy one-bedroom only two hours from the city center, where you can secure a stable and secure job as a key grip in the ever-growing film industry of Vancouver (a.k.a. Hollywood North). Or perhaps you could open a daycare center/funeral home to support the abundant demographic in the capital city of Victoria, home of the newly wed and the nearly dead.

## DOES CANADA HAVE A CAPITAL?

Yes and no. Unlike the U.S., Canada does not have a separate district, but rather it has a National Capital Region (NCR) that sits on the border of Ottawa, Ontario, and Gatineau, Québec, and is overseen by the National Capital Commission (NCC). Ottawa is officially the nation's capital, and it's there you'll find Canada's seat of government and favorite tourist attraction, Parliament Hill, which houses the Canadian Senate and House of Commons.

## MANITOBA (MB)

**POPULATION**–1,282,000

**CAPITAL AND LARGEST CITY**–Winnipeg

**OFFICIAL LANGUAGE**–English

**A.K.A.** Friendly Manitoba, the Keystone Province, the Postage Stamp Province, Land of a 100,000 Lakes. You could also call it a Winter Wonderland (with the right prescription).

Do you enjoy ice fishing? Skating? Skiing? Hours upon hours of indoor activities while praying you have enough firewood to make it through winter? Did your kids really like Disney's *Frozen*? Do you want to build a snowman? If you answered *yes* to any of these questions, you are probably one of the really nice and passive-aggressive folk of the American heartland. If this is true, Manitoba is the place you want to be.

Minnesota only boasts 10,000 lakes, while Manitoba claims more than 100,000. Take that, Minnesota! That's 100,000 semi-treacherous ice rinks in your very own backyard during the winter and 100,000 possibilities for that same backyard flooding during the summer.

If you want to live in one of the few places where snowblowers are sold with odometers and your home can suddenly learn to swim, then you need to be in Manitoba. After all, you can't spell *nice* without *ice.*

# NEW BRUNSWICK (NB)

**POPULATION**—753,900

**CAPITAL**—Fredericton

**LARGEST CITY**—Saint John

**OFFICIAL LANGUAGES**—English and French

**A.K.A.** the Picture Province, the Loyalist Province, the Drive-Through Province. Some refer to it as "Y'know, that place with the boats where we had lobster."

If you're one of those British sympathizers who've harbored a grudge since losing the Revolutionary War, then joining your fellow British loyalists in the province of New Brunswick might suit your need for belonging.

New Brunswick has plenty of picture-perfect scenery to gawk at as you drive to Nova Scotia. If you stop to ask a nice old man for directions, be prepared. Chances are he's an unemployed fisherman and he'll probably answer in French. Don't be fooled, though. He knows how to speak English; he just won't. That's how things are in Nouveau Brunswick.

# NEWFOUNDLAND AND LABRADOR (NL)

**POPULATION**–527,000

**CAPITAL AND LARGEST CITY**–St. John's

**OFFICIAL LANGUAGE**–English

**A.K.A.** the Rock, the Big Land. Canadians know it as the butt of 95 percent of their jokes.

Do you consider yourself an underdog? Have you found yourself laughing at a joke you don't understand just so everyone else won't think you're a bit dense? Has anyone unfairly referred to you or your family as inbred, dimwitted, or "precious"? Are you only pretending to read this book when in reality you're only grinning thoughtfully at the pictures? If you think Newfoundland and Labrador were named after dog breeds, then this might be the province for you.

Pack up the Budget rent-a-truck, grab your cousin (the pretty one), and head north and to the right toward your new trailer-home-sweet-trailer-home. As a newbie "Newfie" you can find work in fishing, fish packing, and fish canning, while living in the fish sticks.

With just about any college degree, you can set up a law or medical practice in the shed out back, and with a master's degree, you're allowed to put a sign out front.

So, if you're looking for a fresh new start in a place where hip waders are considered formal wear and drunkenese is taught as a second language, then Newfoundland and Labrador are the dog breeds for you.

# NOVA SCOTIA (NS)

**POPULATION**—942,700

**CAPITAL AND LARGEST CITY**—Halifax

**OFFICIAL LANGUAGE**—English

A.K.A. the Sea Bound Coast, the Land of Evangeline, Canada's Ocean Playground, Bluenoser Province. The place the lox are named after.

Have you ever had the urge to wear a kilt and get into a bar brawl, beating your opponent with a dead cod while accompanied by a fiddle player? Then Nova Scotia is right up your alley.

This maritime province is an Atlantic peninsula that some locals proudly claim resembles a penis.

Apparently many of the locals have not actually encountered a healthy penis, hence the comparison.

Phallic or not, Nova Scotia has a delightful history of premature evacuation, with hoards of French settlers escaping British rule to settle in the swamplands of Louisiana. If you are one of those festive and fun Cajun folk adored and exploited by the 200 cable channels dedicated to cooking and alligator wresting, then perhaps it's time for you to consider reclaiming Nova Scotia as your rightful home.

After all, what could possibly make Nova Lox better than a touch of Cajun hot sauce?

# ONTARIO (ON)

**POPULATION**–13,678,700

**CAPITAL AND LARGEST CITY**–Toronto

**OFFICIAL LANGUAGE**–English

**A.K.A.** the Heartland Province, the Province of Opportunity. Its license plate reads, "Yours to Discover." What you'll discover is that $2,000 a month will get you a really crappy apartment.

Did you grow up in a big city? New York? Chicago? Boston? Los Angeles? Do you like the hustle and bustle of the rat race and the true grit of city dwelling? Do you want to move to Canada but fear you'll miss the murder and crime rates back in the States?

Well, friend, you can have the best of both worlds in Canada's center of the universe, mother of Canadian commerce, Ontario.

Much like your former homeland's "Big Apple," Ontario's crowded capital, Toronto, offers all the amenities of urban dwelling with nearly half the excitement. Imagine New York City with a healthy addiction to Xanax. If you want to wake up in a city that never forgets to get at least eight hours of sleep on a weekday and at least ten on weekends and holidays, then you, my friend, are in for a real treat.

With an abundance of opportunities in every back alley, you could follow in the footsteps of such famous Torontonian as creator of *SNL* Lorne Michaels, comic actor Jim Carrey, and *The Sound of Music*'s Captain Von Trapp, Christopher Plummer. Can you feel the excitement and promise in the possibility that you, too, could find fame and fortune as the next Ace Ventura? Like the license plate of Ontario says, it's "Yours to Discover."

## PRINCE EDWARD ISLAND (PE)

**POPULATION**–146,300

**CAPITAL AND LARGEST CITY**–Charlottetown

**OFFICIAL LANGUAGE**–English

**A.K.A.** Spud Island, Million Acre Farm, the Garden of Gulf, Abegweit, Minegoo, the Island, the Cradle of Confederation. It's the place where Anne had Green Gables and boiled little red potatoes.

Have you ever dreamed about living on a quaint little island in a quaint little house on a quaint little farm? Does your closet contain a sweatshirt or two that feature kittens in adorable repose? Perhaps there is a romantic novel at your bedside with a single withered rose pressed between the yellowed pages to serve as a reminder that you are mysteriously intriguing with unspoken yet provocative passions.

Can you hear the alluring call? The one that whispers your name after downing that bottle of Ménage à Trois chardonnay and licking the chocolaty flakes from the bottom of an empty Whitman's Sampler box. She is Prince Edward Island. She beckons, "Come, my sweet. Be with me. Scale my fish. Peel my potatoes. Make me whole again. I want you inside me." Don't keep her waiting. In the land of seven gables, one is being reserved just for you.

## QUÉBEC (QC)

**POPULATION**—8,214,700

**CAPITAL**—Québec City

**LARGEST CITY**—Montréal

**OFFICIAL LANGUAGE**—French

**A.K.A.** Je Me Souviens (I Remember), La Belle Province (the Beautiful Province). Also known as the Land of a Thousand Frowns and a Million Cigarette Butts.

## WHAT'S THE DEAL WITH QUÉBEC?

Honestly, most Quebecers are very nice people and are quite contented to call themselves Canadians and live in peace. Beginning in the 1700s, when the French lost their territory to the British, there's been a great deal of contention between the Francophones and the Anglophones of Canada. Threats of separation by an aggressive minority party, the Bloc Québécois, keep the Canadian parliament a bit on edge and continue to stir many heated debates. As a result, Québec has become much like that family member we all have that seems to create a lot of drama at every family gathering and then pouts outside while puffing angrily on a cigarette.

In order to determine whether Québec is the right province for you, here's an easy-to-follow flowchart.

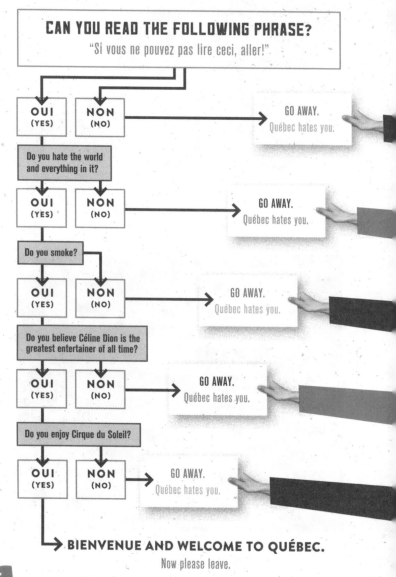

**CAN YOU READ THE FOLLOWING PHRASE?**
"Si vous ne pouvez pas lire ceci, aller!"

**OUI**
(YES)

**NON**
(NO)

GO AWAY.
Québec hates you.

Do you hate the world and everything in it?

**OUI**
(YES)

**NON**
(NO)

GO AWAY.
Québec hates you.

Do you smoke?

**OUI**
(YES)

**NON**
(NO)

GO AWAY.
Québec hates you.

Do you believe Céline Dion is the greatest entertainer of all time?

**OUI**
(YES)

**NON**
(NO)

GO AWAY.
Québec hates you.

Do you enjoy Cirque du Soleil?

**OUI**
(YES)

**NON**
(NO)

GO AWAY.
Québec hates you.

**BIENVENUE AND WELCOME TO QUÉBEC.**
Now please leave.

# SASKATCHEWAN (SK)

**POPULATION**—1,125,400

**CAPITAL**—Regina (pronounced so that it rhymes with *vagina*)

**LARGEST CITY**—Saskatoon

**OFFICIAL LANGUAGE**—English

**A.K.A.** Land of the Living Skies, the Bread Basket of Canada, the Wheat Province, the Land of Seed and Honey. John Deere's Mecca.

This is not a province for the gluten-intolerant. There is wheat here. Lots and lots of wheat. It covers most of the land—the very, very flat land. If you need to borrow a cup of sugar from your neighbor, prepare a week's provisions before you set out on foot. If you enjoy silent solitude and watching little things grow, then Saskatchewan will provide a bucolic life filled with the most miniscule moments of beauty that would drive the sanest person to utter madness. But not you. Oh, no. You are a roughrider. You are from hearty stock. You will spend evenings watching Netflix, practicing taxidermy, and drafting poignant and beautifully lettered suicide notes. This is life as it should be. This is Saskatchewan.

# THE CANADIAN TERRITORIES

## THE NORTHWEST TERRITORIES (NT)

**POPULATION**—41,462

**CAPITAL AND LARGEST CITY**—Yellowknife

**OFFICIAL LANGUAGES**—Chipewyan, Cree, English, French, Gwich'in, Inuinnaqtun, Inuktitut, Inuvialuktun, North Slavey, South Slavey, Tlicho

**A.K.A.** Canada's Last Frontier, Land of the Polar Bear, North of Sixty. Possibly where Santa lives.

If you want to risk freezing to death or being eaten by a hungry polar bear while screaming in hope that one of the 41,000 people who live there (most of whom don't speak a language you can even pronounce) can hear you, then you've found a happy little death trap you can call your own. Get your affairs in order and head north. Way north.

## NUNAVUT (NU)

**POPULATION**—31,906

**CAPITAL AND LARGEST CITY**—Iqaluit

**OFFICIAL LANGUAGES**—English, French, Inuinnaqtun, Inuktitut

**A.K.A.** Our Land, Our Strength. The Land of No Roads. Seriously, how the hell do people get there, and how do they leave?

Keep in mind that the Canadian territories are mostly inhabited by the First Nations of Canada. They are Canada's indigenous people, and they represent the majority in the Territories, particularly Nunavut. They know snow. They know cold. They know how to thrive in the frozen tundra. As a typical American, you probably struggled for survival when Walmart moved to the other side of the suburb. Think carefully before constructing your igloo.

The average temperatures in most of Nunavut will freeze your niblets off. Even the local polar bears have been heard to say, "Fuck this shit!"

# YUKON (YT)

**POPULATION**—33,897

**CAPITAL AND LARGEST CITY**—Whitehorse

**OFFICIAL LANGUAGES**—English and French

A.K.A. the Land of the Midnight Sun.

Frostbite capital of Canada.

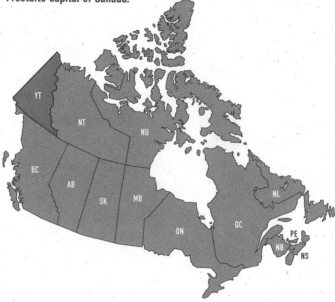

Three months of daylight during the summer followed by three months of darkness during the winter. This is the true test of what one is willing to do for a Klondike bar.

Canada is the second-largest country in the world. At 151,600 miles, Canada has the longest coastline of any country in the world.

# FIND YOUR
# CANADIAN TRAIL

Still ready to kiss 'Murica goodbye? Think you've found the right province or territory that'll sate your uncontrolled hunger for freedom?

Then let's test your knowledge of the Canadian provinces and territories with this fun exercise, shall we?

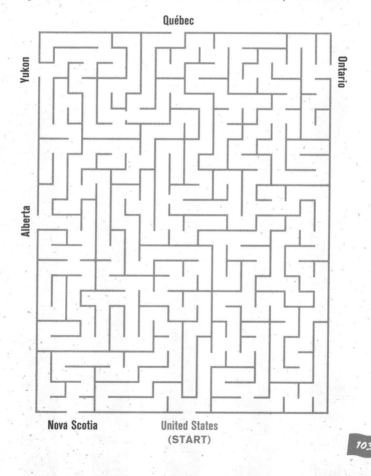

# CHAPTER 6

# PACKING ESSENTIALS AND SYRUP

ongratulations! Your letter of invitation has arrived along with your approved visa. You're all set to flee your homeland like a wussy little puss-wad. But if you're going to be a puss-wad, it's better to be a prepared one. Packing should be your next order of business, and making sure you document everything you've packed will make crossing the border all the less unpleasant for everyone involved. Unless you want the border officers to rifle through every nook and cranny of your personal stuff, and you know one of those boxes has some potentially embarrassing paraphernalia, you'd better have a thorough list of everything you've packed away.

This chapter will hopefully get you thinking ahead about what you'll need to cross the border with confidence, knowing that, even though you are wussing out, you've manned up enough to at least take care of business.

## WHAT STREET IS CANADA ON?

Planning your escape route to Narnia, you'll find you can arrive by land, sea, or air. Either way, you're going to have to go through customs and deal with a border services officer. Make sure the route you choose will have an open border office when you arrive. No, not all offices are open 24/7. Remember, this is Canada, and they respect a healthy work/life balance.

If you are planning on bringing your car, be sure to contact the Registrar of Imported Vehicles (RIV) to ensure your vehicle meets all the required Canadian standards. The Canada Border Services Agency (CBSA) will confirm your vehicle's admissibility, assess duties and taxes, and initiate the RIV registration process. (Note: The fees and taxes can be substantial, so do your homework and be prepared so as to avoid sticker shock.) Once you've entered your province, you'll need to have an RIV inspection (another fee) and complete any modifications needed to be in compliance with Canadian motor vehicle standards (possibly more money). Once that's in order, you can contact your provincial licensing bureau to obtain a proper license. (Yes, there are fees for those too.) You'll be glad to know, though, that most U.S. drivers can simply turn in their driver's license for a Canadian Class 5-GDL license with a simple test of Canadian traffic laws and protocol (yes, another fee, but it's a wee one). Now, wasn't that fun? Wait till you see the price of gas.

## DOCUMENTATION— WELL, I DECLARE!

"May I see your papers?" is an all too familiar catch-phrase in just about any Hollywood film that involves crossing a border. It's also quite accurate. Be prepared for any given situation. Bring your passport, your driver's license, and any correspondence with the Canadian immigration office, potential employers, or Canadian relatives. Have your birth certificate and copies of bills, receipts, medical and school records, car registration, professional certificates or licenses, tax filings, and a comprehensive list of everything you have packed away in the U-Haul (serial and model numbers if available) and anything you have being delivered later along with its value. Even better, complete Form BSF186—Personal Effects Accounting Document before you arrive to speed up the process. Anyone traveling with you will have to show the same personal documents including children, and make sure you can prove those kids are yours.

If you are carrying more than $10,000 in any asset form, be sure to declare it, and know that you may need to pay duty on alcohol, tobacco, or gifts, which, of course, you must declare or face some pretty stiff penalties. If you're in doubt as to what you should declare, err on the side of TMI. Perhaps they'll get tired of hearing you talk about your stuff and just let you in.

Canadians are known for their friendliness, but the unfriendly ones tend to become border services officers. Don't mess with them. Don't write "Explosives" on the side of any of your moving boxes. They won't appreciate the irony. When they ask you if you have anything to declare, don't respond with "I'm not wearing any underwear." That's a surefire way to get a cavity search. Fetching the glove, they'll explain the exam is digital, but you'll be shocked at how excruciatingly analog it really is.

Gather all of these documents, and make dupli-
cates just in case. If you think entering Canada is
difficult, the rules for returning to the U.S. are even
harsher, and nearly all the U.S. border officers will
remind you of that cousin no one really likes.

## WHAT ABOUT PETS?

If you plan on transporting Spot, Rex, or Princess
Pussykins across the border, be prepared with their
papers as well. Cats and dogs require a rabies vaccination certificate from your vet. If you cannot supply
this, then border control will likely require that you
have your pet vaccinated by a certain date with the
record of vaccination turned in to the Canadian Food
Inspection Agency. No, they don't eat cats or dogs
in Canada, but it's rumored Tim Hortons is updating
its menu. You may also have to submit your pet to
a visual inspection by the officer to make sure it's
not showing any signs of illness. If your pet's name
is Foamy, you might have to bribe the officer. Just
sayin'. Make sure you declare your pet's food, which
cannot be in excess of 44 lbs. You must also agree
not to feed any Canadian animals from your pet's

supply. Dogs in Montréal would probably just spit it out before lighting another cigarette anyway. Pet food regulations in Canada are different than those in the States, so keep your kibble to yourself.

If you have a pet amphibian or reptile whose species has been previously introduced to Canada, you're good to go, as long as it's not a turtle or a tortoise. Apparently you can transport a 12-foot crocodile without any issues, but turtles and tortoises can potentially carry salmonella or other serious diseases. To transport these, you'll need to complete an Application for Permit to Import at least thirty days prior to crossing the border.

* If you are traveling with your fish, you'll need to fill out the Importer's Declaration of Ownership for Pet Aquatic Animals Form. *Good luck convincing the border services officer it's your service pet.*

* Birds? *If you've owned Tweety for more than ninety days, you shouldn't have a problem. Just expect to sign a declaration form stating so.*

* What about my fox, raccoon, or skunk? *Who the hell are you? Pocahontas? No. They're not permitted, but you can bring your ferret if he's had his shots.*

* Could I ride in on my horse? *Don't see why not. Just make sure you have an export certificate*

from the USDA and something to clean up his horse-doodles.

* My pet monkey? *Hell-to-the-no. Are you some kind of mad scientist or eccentric pop star? No primates!*

* My rabbit? *They're cute and delicious when properly prepared. No problem.*

* My hamster, guinea pig, and selection of other rodents? *As long as they are not a prairie dog, a Gambian pouch rat, a squirrel, or from Africa, you're probably OK. (Canadians don't like squirrels because of their excessive drug use. Seriously, have you ever watched one try to cross a street?)*

* My scorpion, spider, or other multi-legged friend? *This is tricky. Canadians love their agriculture far more than you love your creepy pet, and they are wary of allowing anything into their country that could present a problem. These sorts of imports are on a case-by-case basis.*

Keep in mind, if you are transporting a pet across the border, you are considered an importer, and as an importer, the burden of following the rules falls on your shoulders. Make sure you have all the paperwork in order so that you and your pet don't end up being detained in quarantine and subjected to a lot of unnecessary and invasive swabbing.

# WHAT ABOUT MY GUNS AND AMMO?

OK, here we go. As stated in a previous chapter, Canadians have guns, and possession of firearms with a proper license is acceptable. Canadians, however, are not crazy about the idea of more guns as a solution to controlling gun violence. Canada has vast tracts of wilderness and is considered by many to be a sportsman's paradise. Thousands of Americans flock to the Canadian forests to witness the majesty of nature and return home with a corpse or two strapped to their roof. If you want to transport your arsenal across the Canadian border, then there are some rules you're going to have to follow.

You'll need to complete a Non-Resident Firearm Declaration (form RCMP 5589) prior to arrival. Don't sign it, though. Your signature will have to be witnessed by the border services officer. If you have more than three firearms, then I'm sorry about the size of your genitals, and you'll also need to complete a continuation sheet. You will pay a fee of CAN$25 and present your firearms for inspection. Large-capacity magazines, even if their intended device is accepted, may be prohibited. So, don't enter Canada like some half-crazed Rambo. Also, don't transport any replica firearms that look like they could be potentially real. This can lead to a lot of unwanted attention and peace-keeping bullets headed your way.

Know that your firearms require a locking device so that they cannot be inadvertently discharged. Upon arrival in your new home, the firearm must be kept in a locked cabinet or place difficult to break into, and the ammunition must be kept separated from the firearm. If kept in an unattended vehicle, the firearm must be kept out of sight in the trunk and the vehicle must be locked. If this sounds like common sense, it's probably because it is.

Your firearm declaration will act as your license, but it is only valid for sixty days and must be renewed before it expires. But hey, you're becoming a perma-nent resident, right? Once you're settled, you'll need to apply for a five-year Possession and Acquisition License (PAL). You'll have to provide evidence that you've completed and passed the written and practical tests for the Canadian Firearms Safety Course. If you think you can pass these tests without taking the course, you're welcome to try. The Chief Firearms Officer of your province or territory can help you set this up and complete a background check. Happy shooting, and try not to put an eye out.

# WINTER SURVIVAL— WHAT TO BRING

Canadian winters can be harsh and long. When you find yourself positively giddy and breaking out Bermuda shorts because the thermometer reads −7, you know you're in for some serious cold. Be sure you're prepared.

Here's a list of some of the items you may or may not have thought about needing to survive. Happy shopping:

- **Long johns and/or thermal underwear.** They're not sexy, but neither are frostbitten genitals.
- **Fleece, fleece, fleece.** Buy a sheep if you have a large family or a really furry cat if it's just you.
- **Insulated leggings,** or just don't shave.
- **Down jackets or overcoats.** You might want to add a few geese to go with that sheep.
- **Hats.** Warm ones. Pretend you're Sherlock Holmes looking for clues that spring will eventually return.
- **Insulated boots with a good tread.** That ground is slippery, and you might not have your government-sponsored health care yet.
- **Socks.** Thin cotton or cashmere ones. Believe it or not, thick ones don't insulate as well.
- **Sunglasses.** Snow produces glare, and at least

this way you'll be able to see yourself sliding off the road and into the frozen lake.

- **Gloves.** Good ones. Yes, they make texting difficult, but so does losing your fingers to frostbite.

- **Crampons.** They may sound like improperly inserted tampons, but in reality they are removable metal cleats that fit over your shoes and allow you to traverse ice.

- **Snowshoes.** Keep a pair of them and a safety kit in your car. Canada has too many tragic "lost on the way to church" stories. Don't be one of them.

- **Heated mattress pad.** They even make them so each side of the bed can be set to a different temperature. This innovation has saved a lot of marriages.

- **Dry wood and a warm and cozy fireplace.** Marshmallows and a Barry White CD sold separately.

- **Headphone earmuffs.** You can keep your ears warm and drown out your whining family pleading as to why you dragged them to this frozen hellhole.

- **Candles, canned goods, snacks, booze, and condoms,** just in case of power outages.

- **Rock salt.** You're going to need to put this down if you want to get in or out of your driveway, and don't put it on popcorn. Just don't. Make sure you wash your car a couple of times during the winter. Otherwise the salt will eat the paint right off your vehicle.

* **Ice chest.** This may sound stupid, but if you just put the contents of your fridge out in the snow, you may wake up to polar bears passed out next to your Hyundai.

* **Remote car starter.** This will warm up your car and may even scare off the polar bears. But don't count on it.

It's happening. It's really happening. You're making the move. Good for you. Soon you'll be watching America collapse upon itself in a wave of inconsolable grief following your abrupt departure. But you won't care. You're a resident of Canada now. You'll stand just and proud on the fertile soil of your new homeland and solemnly think to yourself, "Oh shit, I think my feet are frozen to the ground."

# CIRCLE THE USEFUL WINTER GEAR TO PACK

Identify the gear that will keep you warm and alive as opposed to the useless American gear you currently own.

# CHAPTER

# 7

# MAKING THE LEAP

o, you went through with it? You've kicked America to the curb and are now knee-deep in Canadian soil. You've sampled poutine, drunk your weight in Molson, told a Newfie joke or two, and even found yourself adding *eh?* to the end of just about every question. You are assimilating. Just go with it. You are going through the process of Canadafication. Just don't be tempted to call yourself a Canuck yet. There are a few things still left for you to attend to. This chapter will guide you through some of the last steps you'll need to take to becoming a full-fledged, elk-jerky-eating, flannel-wearing, maple-syrup-dripping Canadian.

# GET A JOB, YOU HOSER

If you didn't secure a job before you arrived, you are in for quite a treat. With an unemployment rate of 7.2 percent, which is bound to skyrocket once the American economy collapses with the loss of your talents and skills, you are going to have to make finding gainful employment your full-time occupation.

Be proactive in your approach. Register with the Canadian government's Job Bank (which you can do on its website). There you will find a multitude of opportunities waiting for someone with mad experience just like you. You could make $13.00 an hour as a dishwasher in Alberta or $375,000 a year as a gynecologist in Labrador. You could offer poetry therapy classes at the local community college in Vancouver or set up a veterinarian psychology clinic for neurotic shih tzus in Victoria. Just know that you are not a genuine Canuck yet, and employers are bound to show favoritism for their fellow citizens. Don't let that stop you, though. Make sure you have your work permit in hand, along with your SIN card (even temporary residents can get one of these), multiple copies of your résumé, and diplomas or certifications, strap on a fresh pair of crampons, and hit the pavement with confident gusto.

By the way, some employers may not accept your educational credentials if they were not earned in Canada. You may also encounter a few challenges with language requirements, depending on your mastery of English, French, or both. Some employers may also take issue with your lack of experience in the Canadian workforce. Don't be deterred, though. Flash that smile, shake your moneymaker—whatever part of your body you think that might be—and flex your charm muscle. Do it with humility, though. Remember, Canadians don't appreciate braggers.

Here's a bit of good news. The Canadian minimum wage is set by each of the ten provinces and three territories with the lowest hourly wage set for gratuity earners in Québec at $9.05 to the highest hourly wage set at $13.00 in Nunavat. Not great, but better than most U.S. states.

## DO CANADIANS REALLY PAY MORE TAXES?

This is a complicated question, and the best answer is, "It depends." The U.S. federal income tax rate is set between 10 and 35 percent for individuals, while

Canada's is 15 to 33 percent. The U.S. rate bumps up to 25 percent when an individual earns a yearly gross of $37,451, while the Canadian rate stays at 15 percent until $45,282. This is often cited as the reason lower-income Canadians are a bit better off than lower-income Americans.

But wait, there's more. Unlike some U.S. states that do not impose a state tax, all provinces and territories in Canada do. Canadians also pay an Employment Insurance (EI) premium of 1.88 percent with the employer matching the employee's contribution 1.4 times. The maximum an employee pays in annual premiums is set at a little under $1,000, though.

In the U.S., you could pay up to a maximum of 15.3 percent into the Federal Insurance Contributions Act (FICA), which covers Social Security and Medicare, with half that amount covered by your employer if you're not self-employed. In Canada, there is the Canadian Pension Plan (CPP), which levies an annual contribution rate of 4.95 percent from the employee and is matched by the employer with a maximum annual contribution of $2,544.30 from both. With Canada's national healthcare program, there is no need for Medicare service, so this fund is solely for citizen's retirement. There's also a national supplemental pension plan not so delicately named the Old Age Security Program. No surprise, Québec doesn't participate in the CPP, supporting its own similar program, the QPP, with has slightly higher rates. As stated before—Québec is a pain in the derriere.

Let's not forget about health care. The average U.S. citizen can pay between $2,500 and $5,000 in annual healthcare premiums, not including copays, deductibles, and additional family member premiums. Canadians have equal access to practitioners, procedures, and facilities paid through their annual taxation.

So, will you pay more taxes as a Canadian? You'll have to determine the answer yourself, as you know your financial situation better than anyone. It'll depend on how much you make, where you live, and what benefits and deductions are at your disposal.

But, like they say, money can't buy happiness, eh? Although, like a keg, it can certainly be rented.

## READY TO BECOME A CITIZEN?

As a Permanent Resident Card–carrying expat, you are ready to take that final step. You've learned to love Canadian culture and tolerate Canadian winters. You've listened to Céline Dion and Justin Bieber and thought to yourself, "Hey, I could dance to this." You've taken in a Cirque de Soleil show and weren't completely freaked out by the world's most unfunny clowns. You've downed a two-four of Labatt with a bud or two, followed by a mop at Tim Hortons, ending with horking a semi-digested BeaverTail in the parkade next to McDicks. You find yourself feeling less entitled and more community-driven, seeking consensus and trying not to rock the boat while still searching for opportunities to "rock the canoe." Like an American caterpillar, you are about to emerge from the cage of your chrysalis and spread your wings as a beautiful and brilliant, yet humble-to-the-core, Canadian butterfly.

Before you pop out of your pupa, though, you still have a few details to attend to and some big questions to ask yourself and your family.

## DO I HAVE TO RENOUNCE MY U.S. CITIZENSHIP?

No. Canada allows dual citizenship, but you could potentially lose your Canadian citizenship if convicted of certain crimes. Promise to be good, eat your vegetables, brush your teeth, and don't forget to floss. Promise these and you can stay Canadian.

## DO I HAVE TO PAY TAXES IN BOTH COUNTRIES?

If Canada is your home base and where your income is earned, you will pay taxes in Canada. There are protections to prevent double taxation, but you'll have to figure that out with your tax advisor. This book is far too cheap to be doling out tax advice. Find a professional or buy a bigger book.

## WILL I LOSE MY SOCIAL SECURITY BENEFITS?

This is a bit complicated, much like the Social Security Administration. You can ask but probably will in fact lose them. There are a number of rules and quite a bit of paperwork that need to be followed and completed to maintain benefits for yourself and/or your survivors.

In general, it's cute you think there will be Social Security payouts much further into America's future.

# I WANT TO BE A BONA FIDE CANUCK. WHAT DO I DO?

Although you do not need a Permanent Resident Card to apply as a citizen, it certainly helps speed up the process. In order to be eligible for Canadian citizenship, you must have resided in Canada for 1,460 days during the six years prior to submitting your application. You must show proof that you've met your tax filing obligations for four of the six years prior to submitting your application. You must declare your intent to reside in Canada. You need to prove your proficiency in English or French. You must provide evidence of your understanding of Canadian rights, responsibilities, and privileges of citizenship. You must understand Canada's history, values, institutions, and symbols. Oh, and you will be tested, but there's a sixty-eight-page study guide provided on the website, and it's filled with some pretty interesting stuff if you are craving more documentation now that you've finally made it.

Once you've met all the requirements, passed the test, and bought a spiffy new ensemble, you're all set to attend your citizenship ceremony. It's like the Oscars for less attractive people. There you will take the Oath of Canadian Citizenship.

Here, read it aloud. It'll be good practice. Try it in silly voices. That's always fun.

*I swear (or affirm)*
*That I will be faithful*
*And bear true allegiance*
*To Her Majesty*
*Queen Elizabeth the Second*
*Queen of Canada*
*Her Heirs and Successors*
*And that I will faithfully observe*
*The laws of Canada*
*And fulfill my duties*
*As a Canadian citizen.*

You'll then sign the oath form, receive your certificate of citizenship, endure three whacks from the sacred paddle, and be forced to drink directly from the udder of the mythical white moose. *(I may have made some of that up.)*

**Congratulations. You are now a Canadian, a Canuck, a Canajun, a Canuckistanian.**

Some friends and family back in the States may remember you as a whiny, discontented, and pouty American who left with all your toys, but you know the real truth. You went seeking something better, something real. You are a brave and loosely defined pioneer. You have established a new life and a new hope as a discontented and pouty Canadian. Perhaps next year will find you reading *How to Move to Costa Rica: A Frozen Canadian's Guide to Tropical Relocation*.

*Until then, best of luck, eh?*

# COMPLETE YOUR NEW
# NATIONAL ANTHEM

Fill in the blanks to your new favorite song! When searched, can also create a great Pandora station for further research.

*O Canada! Our home and _____ land!*
*True _____ _____ in all thy sons command.*
*With glowing hearts we see thee rise,*
*The True _____ strong and free!*
*From far and wide, O _____,*
*We stand on _____ for thee.*
*God keep our land, glorious and free!*
*O _____, we stand on guard for thee;*
*O Canada, we stand on _____ for thee.*

*O _____! Where pines and _____ grow,*
*Great prairies spread and Lordly rivers flow!*
*How dear to us thy _____ domain,*
*From _____ to Western sea!*
*The land of hope for all who toil,*
*The true _____ strong and free!*
*God keep our _____, _____ and free.*
*O Canada, we stand on guard for thee!*
*O Canada, we stand on guard for thee!*

O Canada! Beneath thy _____ skies,

May _____sons, and gentle maidens rise.

To keep thee steadfast thro' the years,

From East to _____ sea.

Our own beloved native land,

Our true _____ strong and free!

God keep our land, glorious and free.

O _____, we stand on guard for thee!

O Canada, we stand on guard for thee!


Ruler supreme, who _____ humble prayer,

Hold our _____, in thy _____care.

Help us to find, O God, in thee,

A _____ rich reward.

As waiting for the better day,

We ever stand on guard.

God keep our land, glorious and free.

O Canada, we stand on _____for thee!

O _____, we stand on guard for thee!

# ABOUT THE AUTHOR

 Louisiana-born, self-proclaimed word monkey and consummate smart-ass, **André du Broc** has enjoyed a wonderful and wacky life. A retired circus clown, greeting card writer, teacher, actor, and musician, he and his husband, Dan, can see Canada from their home in the frozen tundra of Minnesota, where they live with an assortment of orange tabbies and a case of Kentucky bourbon to provide them warmth. To find out more, go to www.andredubroc.com.

# ACTIVITIES
# ANSWER KEY

Color the Flag of Your New Homeland, page ix:

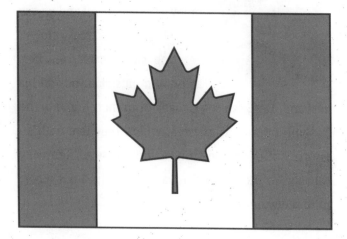

## A Visa-Data Word Search, page 19:

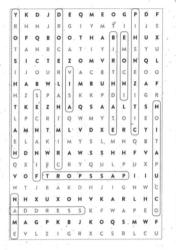

## Find Your Visa Word Search, page 36:

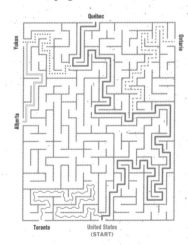

## Match the Words with Their Definitions, page 53:

**chesterfield**
**mickey**
**toonie**
**mountie**
**serviette**
**housecoat**
**Barenaked Ladies**
**stag/stagette**
**girl guide**
**arse**

**ANSWER:**
**Time to move to Canada**

## Find Your Canadian Trail, page 103:

## Circle the Useful Winter Gear to Pack, page 117:

## Complete Your New National Anthem, page 129:

*O Canada! Our home and native land!*
*True patriot love in all thy sons command.*
*With glowing hearts we see thee rise,*
*The True North strong and free!*
*From far and wide, O Canada,*
*We stand on guard for thee.*
*God keep our land, glorious and free!*
*O Canada, we stand on guard for thee;*
*O Canada, we stand on guard for thee.*

*O Canada! Where pines and maples grow,*
*Great prairies spread and Lordly rivers flow!*
*How dear to us thy broad domain,*
*From East to Western sea!*
*The land of hope for all who toil,*
*The true North strong and free!*
*God keep our land, glorious and free.*
*O Canada, we stand on guard for thee!*
*O Canada, we stand on guard for thee!*

*O Canada! Beneath thy shining skies,*
*May Stalwart sons, and gentle maidens rise.*
*To keep thee steadfast thro' the years,*
*From East to Western sea.*
*Our own beloved native land,*
*Our true North strong and free!*
*God keep our land, glorious and free.*
*O Canada, we stand on guard for thee!*
*O Canada, we stand on guard for thee!*

*Ruler supreme, who hearest humble prayer,*
*Hold our Dominion, in thy loving care.*
*Help us to find, O God, in thee,*
*A lasting rich reward.*
*As waiting for the better day,*
*We ever stand on guard.*
*God keep our land, glorious and free.*
*O Canada, we stand on guard for thee!*
*O Canada, we stand on guard for thee!*